Making Merchandise From Art

How to make
t-shirts mugs notecards tote bags
and more
from your artwork

Lisa Shea

CONTENTS

INTRODUCTION

"To create one's own world takes courage."
-- Georgia O'Keeffe

The wealth of options for presenting your art is nearly limitless. There are stores which will create prints for you on metal. On canvas. You can get mugs. T-shirts. Tote bags. Note cards. Christmas cards. Necklaces. The possibilities are nearly endless.

This book steps you through the three main tasks involved in having your art showcased on an item of merchandise.

These are:

- Creating a clear photograph of your artwork, if it is not already a photograph.
- Moving that photograph onto a computer where it is prepared for use.
- Using an online service such as FineArtAmerica.com or CafePress.com to design various merchandise options using that final image.

This book will walk you through each step of that process.

Let's get started!

All proceeds from sales of this book, in locations where it isn't free as intended (for example in paperback format), support childhood art programs.

TAKING A PHOTO OF YOUR ARTWORK

If the artwork you are planning to use is already a photo, then you're all set. You have that image of your artwork. So, for example, if you took this photo of a gazebo at Christmas:

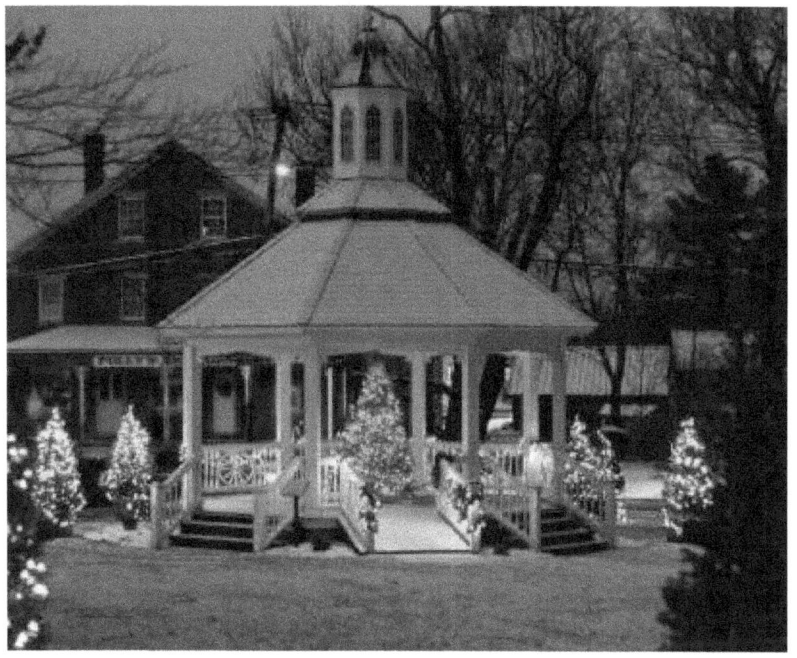

You're all set. You can now move on to the next stage of this process.

However, let's say that you have an acrylic painting you've just created. Or a pen-and-ink drawing. Maybe it was done with watercolors. Whatever this "real life" work of art is, you now need to somehow get it into your computer in a way which best represents what that image looks like in the real world.

Here's how to do that.

USE WHITE LIGHT

You might think that all light is the same. But it's amazing how different it actually is.

The old-style incandescent bulbs, the ones many of us grew up with, aren't white. They actually give off a yellowish light. That means if you take a photo of a painting which is lit by incandescent bulbs, your results will end up looking yellowish.

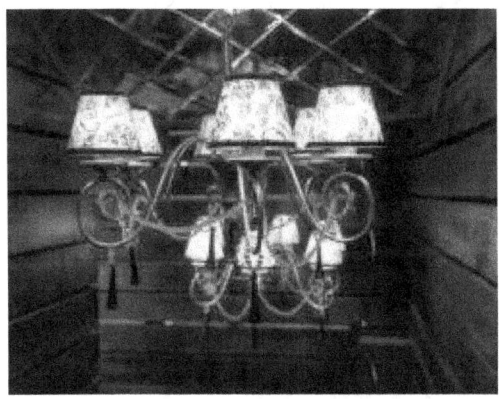

How about fluorescent lights – the kinds that are found in many office buildings? Those have a different kind of challenge. Those lights tend to give off a bluish color, turning your images blue.

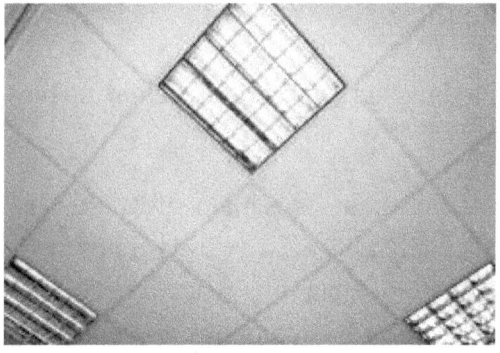

What's the solution?

It's up over your head, at least during the day. The sun. The reason the sun can make rainbows is that it has all colors of visible light in it. Not too blue. Not too yellow. Just right.

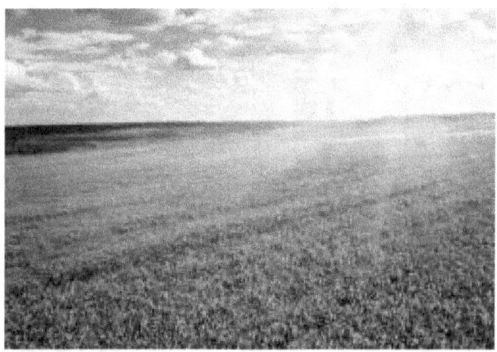

The reason the sun can look yellow, orange, or red when near the horizon is that the atmosphere is impacting it. But the sun is actually white. If you take your photos during the main hours of the day, you're getting pure white light.

If it's really bright out, it's good to take the photo in an area of light, even shade. That way you're not getting the glare of the sun while also avoiding the dark-shadow-across-image issue.

If for some reason you can't take your photos outside with that natural light, you need to find an indoor light that mimics the same effect.

LED lights are one solution. These are naturally white and will not cause a color cast issue with your photography.

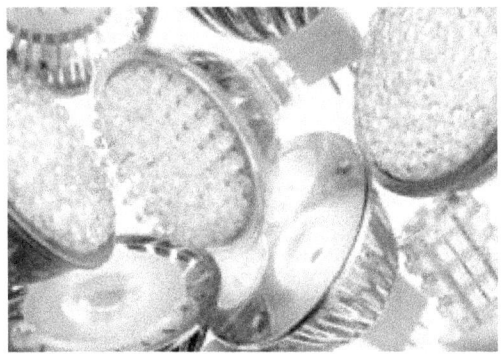

Another solution is to get the "full sunlight bulbs" that they have for plants. These also mimic the sun.

Here's the rig that many people in the Blackstone Valley Art Association use. It is a Husky LED light on stand which lets you position it wherever you wish and illuminate the entire image cleanly.

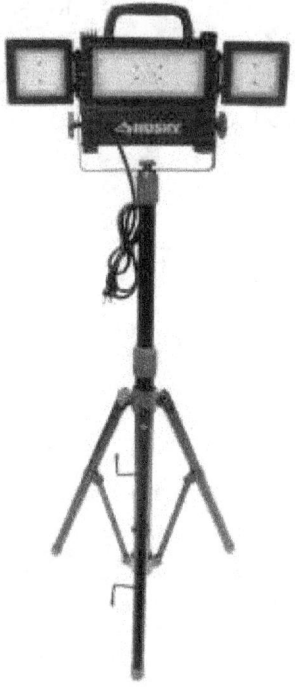

It's currently about $80 at Home Depot. It comes in handy for all sorts of other household projects, too, and is on a five foot stand.

Whatever light you use, it should have the full spectrum of colors in it.

AVOID PINPOINT LIGHT

You want to make sure your light is not a pin-point source like a flashlight or the flash on a camera. If a light comes from just one spot it's likely to create a glare on the image you're taking a photo of. That will show up in the final result and be distracting.

For example, here's a light glare showing up on the glass of an hourglass. It's caused because the light source is small and distinct.

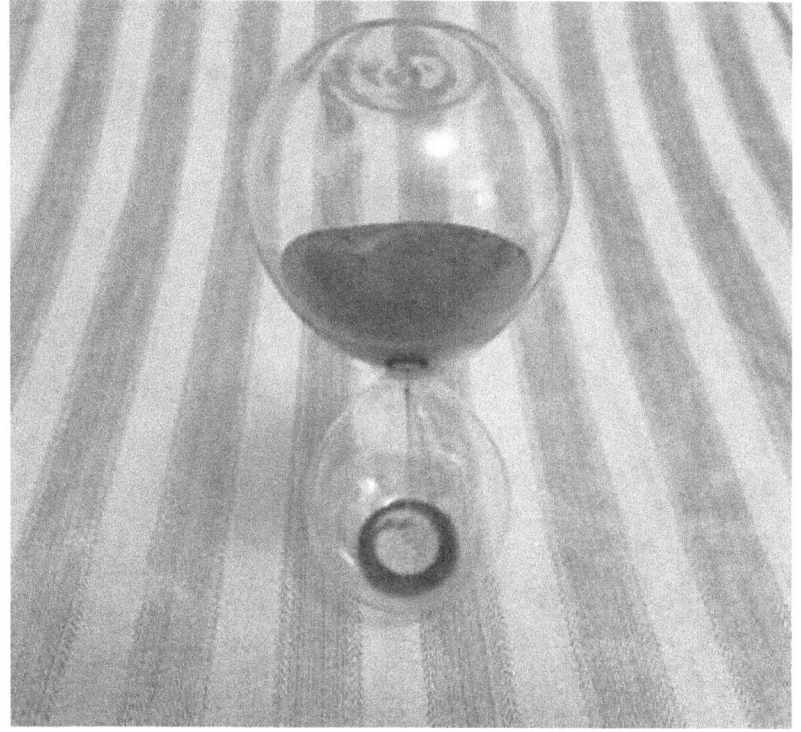

The shinier the surface of your work, the more problems you will get with glare. If you varnish the top of your painting, it could get shiny / glary even with a diffuse light source. It might be wise to photograph your painting before you apply the varnish layer.

Definitely remove any glass frame from your artwork before taking the photo. Glass will cause all sorts of glare and reflection issues.

AVOID SHADOWS

If anything at all gets between your light source and your artwork, it can throw shadows.

Sometimes that is obvious. If your arm is blocking half of the light, that will cast a strange shadow.

Sometimes it's less obvious. If you're taking a photo outside, maybe a tree branch is casting a twisting shadow across your art. It causes subtle variations in the darkness of the image.

Make sure your art is not in any shadow before you take your photo. That way you get an evenly lit surface.

CAMERA SQUARE TO THE IMAGE

You want the image you have in the photograph to be an exact representation of the image in real life. This means you need the front of the camera to be perfectly parallel and in line with the actual artwork.

Here's an example.

Linda DeFeudis created this lovely artwork of a bicycle. However, when I took its photo, I had the camera at a slant to the image. The result is that the image looks trapezoidal.

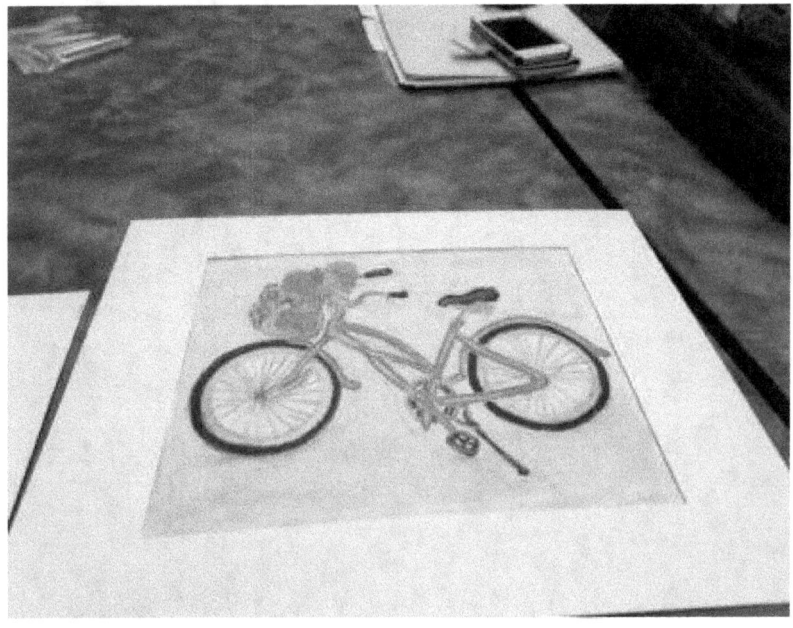

I won't be able to use that on a mug or t-shirt. It doesn't look right.

Instead, I have to make sure the front lens of the camera is perfectly parallel to the artwork itself. I like to put the artwork on the floor and then stand over it with a camera. Other people like to put the camera onto a tripod and then prop the artwork up on a table in front of it. However you choose to do this operation, you need the face of the artwork and the front lens of the camera to be parallel with each other.

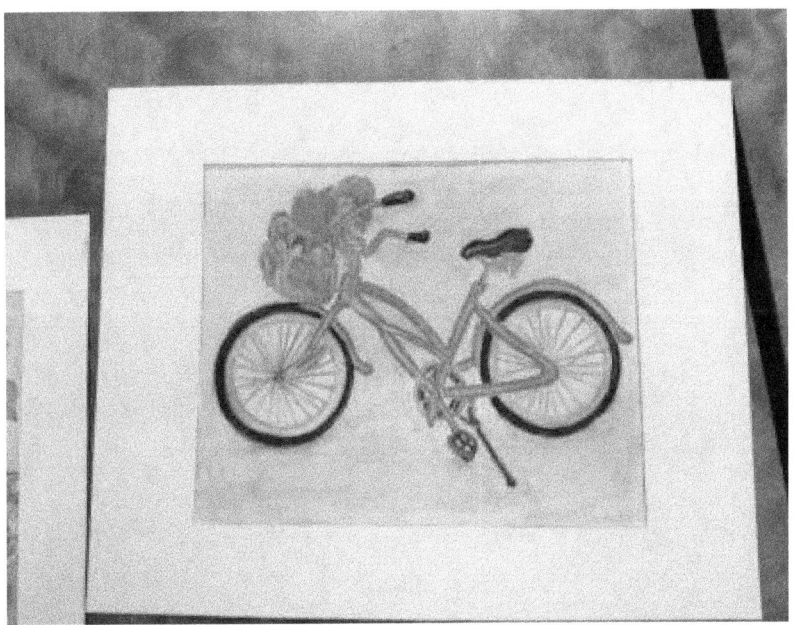

Don't rely on a paint or photo-editing program to fix the proportions for you – those introduce a wealth of other issues. Just take a bunch of photos of the artwork in question and then choose the one which came out the most perfectly square.

Don't worry about the extra background at this stage. We'll handle that later. For now, just aim to have the image itself as square-on as possible.

PHOTO FORMAT

Most inexpensive cameras and cellphones take photos in JPG format. This is a standard photo format that just about every software can handle.

Higher end cameras can also take photos in RAW format. While RAW format is great for high end photography and complex editing, it can only be used by certain software packages.

For the purposes of this book, it's really best to take these photos in JPG format. That way it's nice and simple. The photo you take can instantly be used by the software and companies we are talking about.

If you're not sure which format your camera uses, it's probably using JPG. You can try taking a few photos and then looking at the files on the memory card to see if they end in .RAW or .JPG.

SUMMARY

Your aim here is to get the most perfect representation of your work of art into the computer as possible. This means the color and light should match what the original image had. There shouldn't be aberrant shadows impacting the work. The work should be presented as square-to-the-source as possible, so the image is not unnaturally twisted or stretched.

Once you have that image in your camera or cellphone, it's time to get it into your computer for the next step.

PREPARING YOUR PHOTO FOR USE

You now have a photo in your camera or cellphone. The next step is to get it into your computer / laptop / tablet and prepare it for use in the various online systems.

Here's how to proceed.

CAMERA WITH MEMORY CARD

If your camera has a memory card, you would want to remove the memory card from the camera and insert it into your PC / laptop / etc.

If your machine does not have a slot which fits your memory card, it's probably time to invest in a card reader. These devices typically have a standard USB plug on one end and then let you stick various memory cards into the other end.

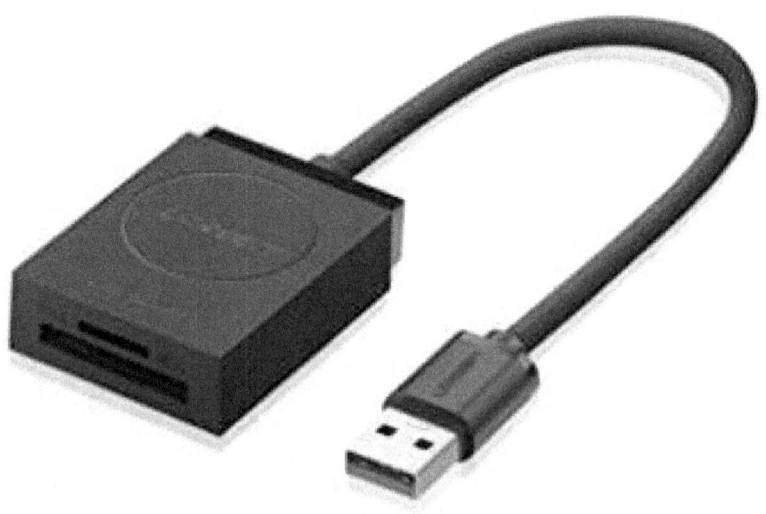

You should always have a way to take your memory card out of your camera and insert into *something* useful, to then get access to those files.

Once your card is accessible to your PC, you should be able to see that card as a "drive" (something like Drive L: or Drive M: or so on) in your normal file management program.

Use that regular File Management program to drag-and-drop the files off of that memory card and into a folder of your choosing. I recommend naming that folder something useful like "LisaPhotos" so that it's easy to find later on.

CELLPHONE CAMERA

Most cellphones come with a cable that lets you connect them to your computer. You plug one end of the cable into your cellphone and the other end into your computer. You should then be able to see the cellphone as a "drive" in your normal file management program.

In some cases your cellphone simply refuses to be seen by your computer. Or maybe you've lost the cable. What I do in cases like this is I open my email program on my cellphone. I then send myself an email and attach the image I want. There should always be an option in email to "add an attachment" – sometimes that option is represented by a paper clip icon.

On my PC, I log into my email. That email message will be there with the image I want. I can then download the image into my "Lisaphotos" folder. You usually download an image by RIGHT clicking on it (not left clicking).

You can also use social networking sites. I can log into Facebook on my cellphone and send a private message to my boyfriend, attaching the image I want. Then I go to my PC. I log into Facebook there and look at my messages. I'll see the image there that I sent to my boyfriend. I can now download it on that PC.

Typically, to download an image you RIGHT click on it (not left click). You'll get options of what to do with it, including saving it.

On my Samsung Android phone I also have free software installed, "AirDroid" which lets me move files from my cellphone to my PC fairly easily. There's probably similar software for other systems.

So there are a variety of ways to get your images off of your cellphone and onto your PC.

If you get stuck with this step, ask me and I'll lend a hand.

EDITING YOUR PHOTO

Once your photo is on your PC, it's time to edit it.

I recommend doing the least amount of editing possible. If your photo angle ended up making your rectangular oil painting into a trapezoid, it's best to re-take the photo. If your incandescent light bulbs turned your Christmas scene into a yellow desert, re-take the photo. Trying to fix those kinds of issues on the computer is likely to cause more harm than good to your image.

There are all sorts of programs out there to edit photos with. Lightroom. Photoshop. But for this book, we'll do the examples in Paint, which comes for free with every Windows-based PC. Apple users can use their copy of iPhoto in just about the same way. If you want to tackle these operations in a more complicated program like Photoshop, it should have the same options but just in different screen locations.

OPENING PAINT

Click on your Windows icon in the lower left of your PC.
Depending on your version of Windows, you may see a folder
right there called 'Accessories' with a link to Paint. On other
versions of Windows you may at first see your most commonly
used programs, and then a down-arrow on the left side to get to
all of the other programs. If that's the case, use the down-arrow
to see all the programs and then find Paint under the 'Windows
Accessories' section.

The icon for Paint looks like a palate with a brush.

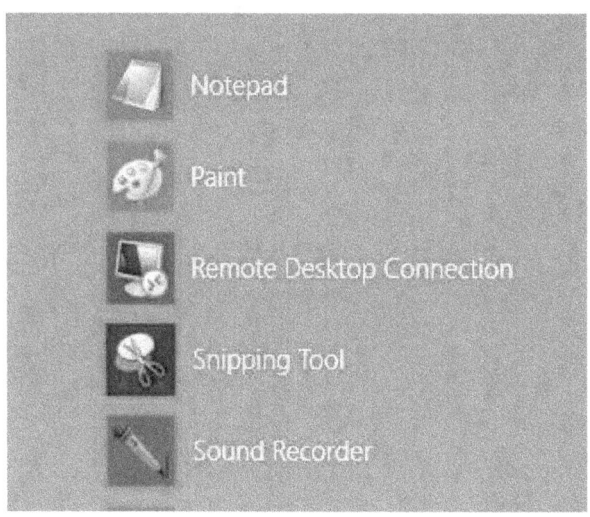

If you can't find your Paint program, email me and I'll help
you figure it out.

Click on the icon to launch paint.

PREPARING YOUR IMAGE

Once Paint is running, click on FILE and then OPEN.

You will be asked to browse your files to select the one you want to work on. Navigate to the folder where you store your photos, and choose the one you'd like.

That image will now be in the Paint program for you to work with.

If you can only see a portion of the image, use the View – Zoom Out option to zoom out until you can see the entire image on your screen.

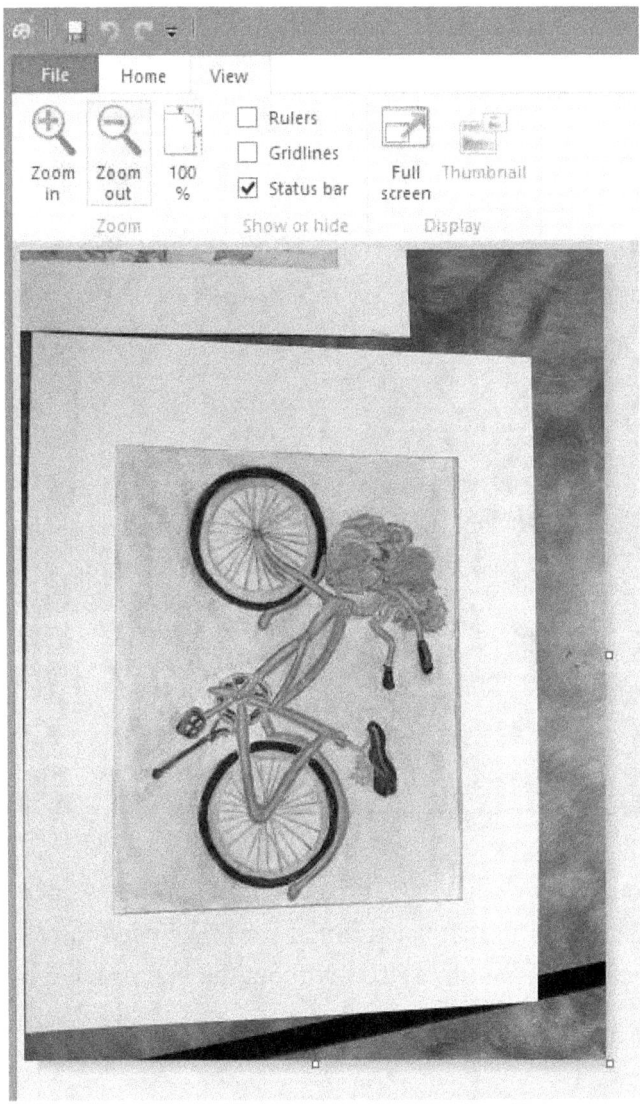

Sometimes the images come in rotated. Use the home – Rotate option to rotate it until it lines up properly.

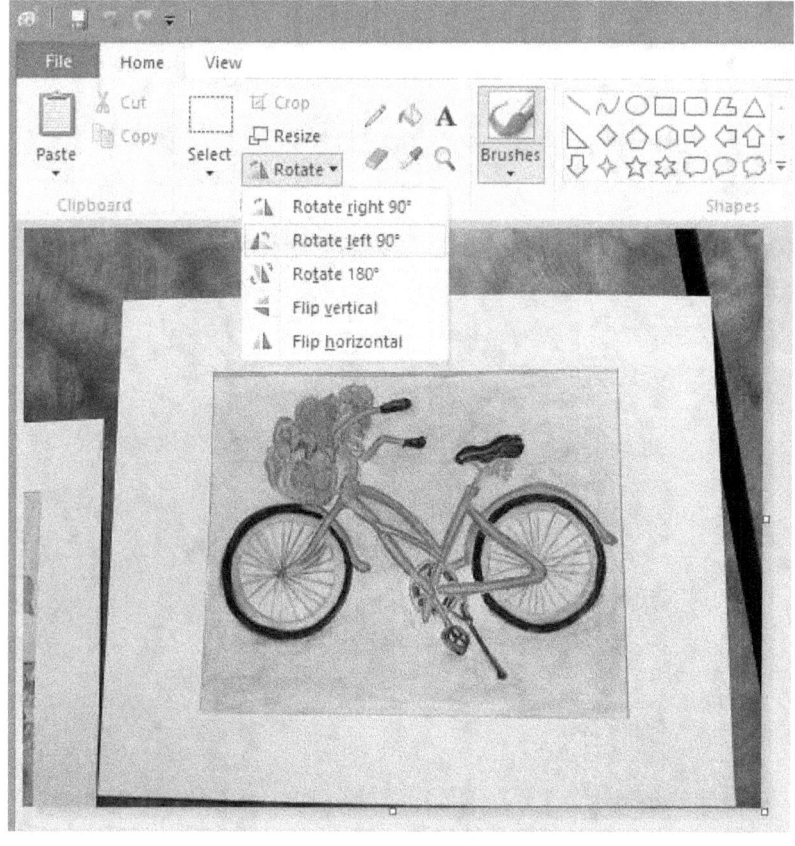

So far so good. Now we have the image looking proper – but we want to get rid of all that background stuff. We need the painting to be just the painting itself without the mat or table or so on.

CROPPING YOUR IMAGE

To select just the painting portion of our file, we are going to crop the image. To crop an image means to select down to just a portion of it.

To start the crop process, click on the "selection" tool. This means your mouse will now act as a means of selecting part of the image. This is in comparison with it acting as a brush.

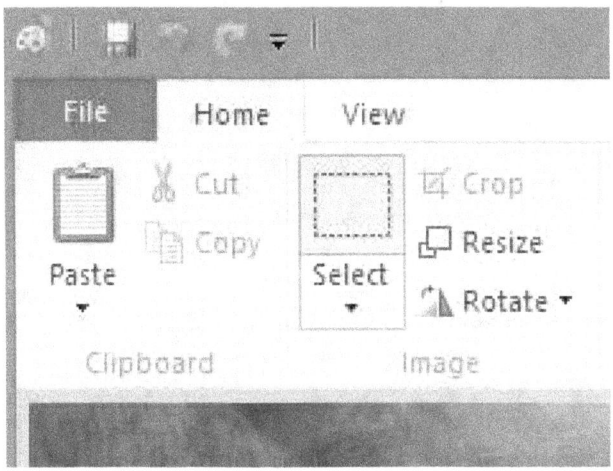

Now that your mouse's clicks will select things, start by clicking and holding at the top left corner of your painting area. While you are holding down the mouse button, move your mouse until the dashed lines surround your painting. If you miss, that's OK. Just click anywhere to reset the selection box and start again. It's fine to take a few tries until you get the hang of this.

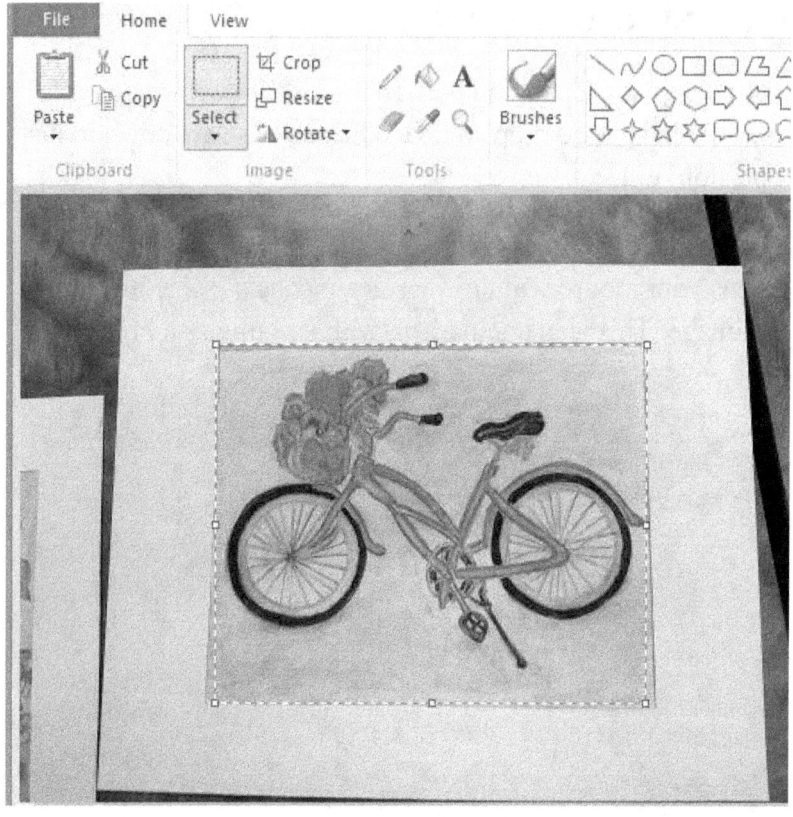

You can see here why it's important to take that photo as straight-on as possible of your artwork. If your image was a trapezoid, you'd be missing out on parts of your artwork when you tried to select it here. The more straight-edged your camera photo of your artwork is, the better this process will work.

If your artwork ended up being slanty in your photo, it's better to go back and retake the photo vs trying to fix it in here.

Once you have a rectangular selection box that you are happy with, click the "crop" button.

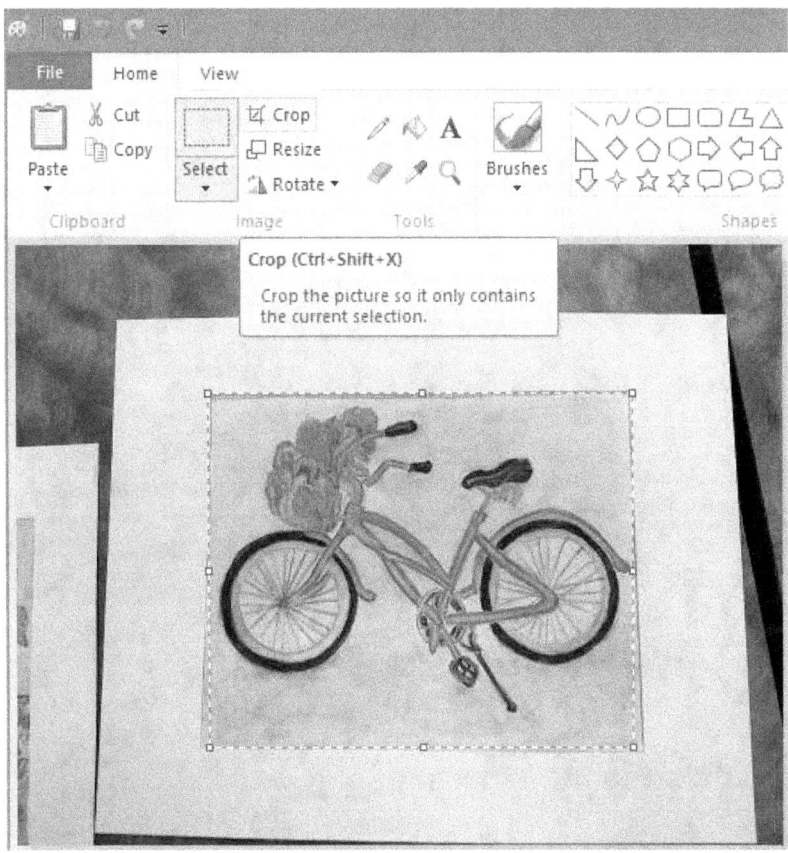

Once you click that button, your image will be cropped to
include just what was within that rectangular selection area.

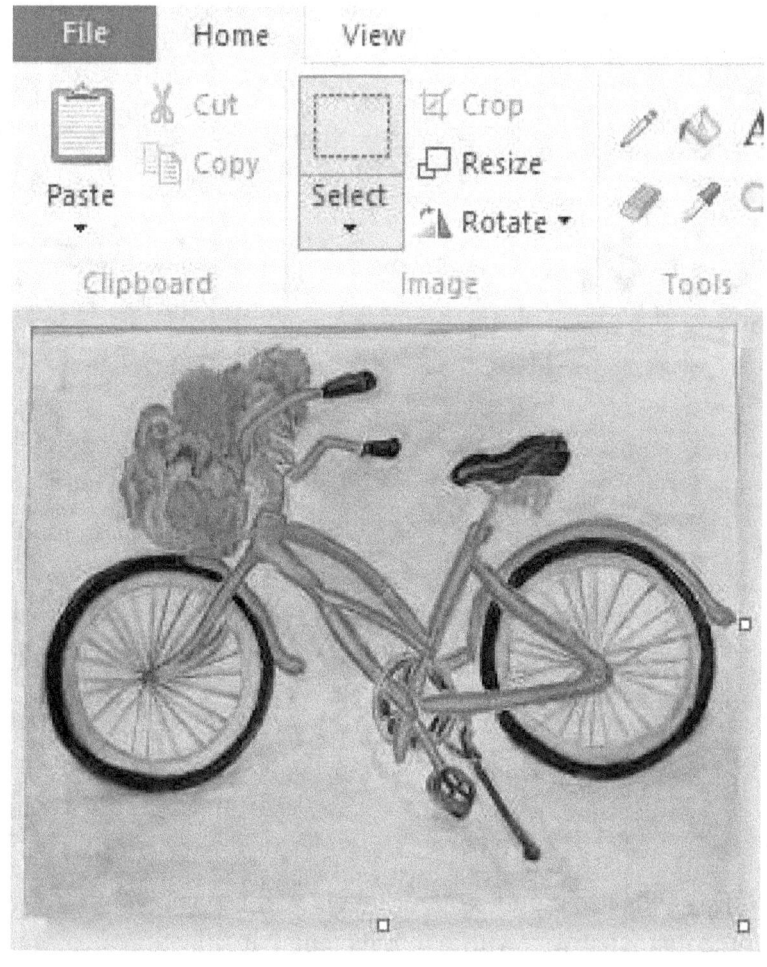

Note that the gray background is just the border edge in Paint – it's not part of the actual image.

If you don't like how the crop worked, just hit the "undo" button (the counter-clockwise blue arrow) and try again.

Once you are satisfied with your crop, use File – Save to save your image under a new name. Give it something you'll remember, like PinkBike.jpg.

JPG VS GIF

Throughout these examples we've been talking about JPG format images, as those are the standard. However, JPG does not allow transparency.

Here's where that might matter.

Let's say you have an image that is oddly shaped. For example, this BVAA logo. It's not a rectangle. It's letters and colors on a background.

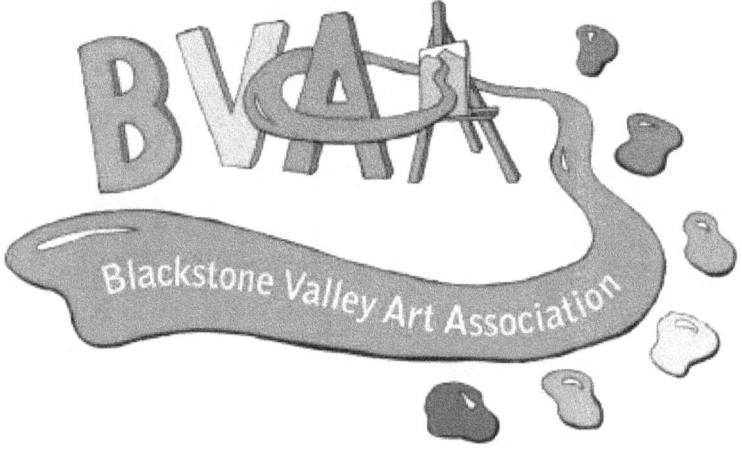

If that had a white background, and you put it on a black t-shirt, you'd end up with a black t-shirt with a white rectangle on it with the words on that white rectangle. That might not look very professional.

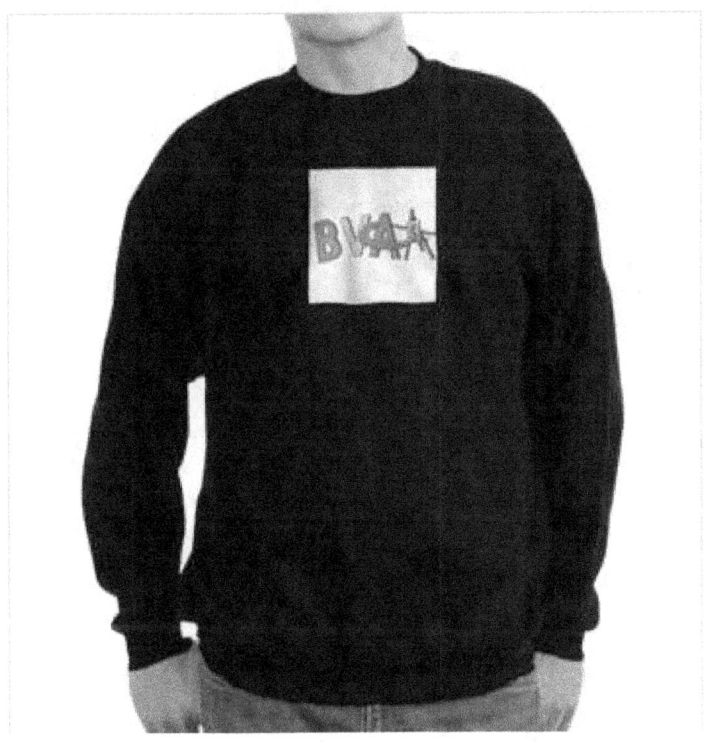

What you'd rather have is an image where there is no
"background". Where the image is just the letters and colors,
against a transparent background. That way the shirt or
whatever shows through in those other areas.

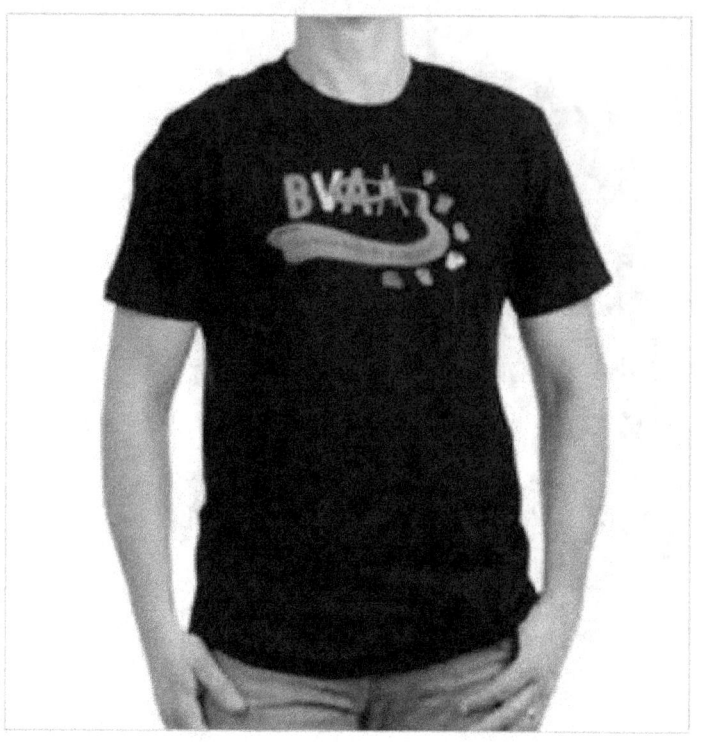

You need to make a GIF to do this. This will take a lot more work and is best done with a tool like PhotoShop. I recommend you ask a friend to help with this, if you're not comfortable watching how-to YouTube videos to step you through the process.

To summarize quickly, for those who understand PhotoShop, what you do is this. You open up the logo (or whatever the art is) and select the background. Hopefully that background is basic white, like in the above example. Then you use Select – Inverse to select everything else on the image besides the background. You should now have the entire logo (sans background) selected. You "copy" that. You create a new file on a transparent background and you "paste" your logo onto that transparent background. You should now have the logo on a transparent background. You then safe that as a GIF and you're all set.

If this is confusing, you can also go to http://Fiverr.com where you can get someone to do it for you for just a few dollars.

In general, just be aware of the transparency issue, if you're working with a logo or other item where you want transparency to happen. That way you know it can be handled.

SUMMARY

Now that you have a nicely cropped image of your painting, you're ready to start using it on the merchandising websites!

FINEARTAMERICA.COM

We'll start with FineArtAmerica.com. This site is geared toward higher priced items, like a giant print to hang over your living room couch. Magazines use this site to find covers. For example, a drawing from FineArtAmerica was used by the New Yorker. You might not get a lot of sales here, but each one might be at a high enough price that it's still worth doing.

It is wholly free to set up an account at FineArtAmerica. If you decide to load more than 25 images into their system they'll charge you an annual fee of $25 for that image storage. It's worth it to set up the free account and to load 24 images into it, to see how this works.

Note this is all print-on-demand. Nothing is printed or made until an order comes in.

To create an account just go to http://www.fineartamerica.com and click "Join" in the top right. You want to create an Artist / Photographer account. You'll put in some basic information like your name, address, email address, and so on.

Once you get those in, you're now able to start loading in your art.

PROFILE SCREEN

This is what a profile screen looks like in FineArtAmerica. It lets you work with your images, arrange collections of images, and do other activities.

My screen below already has some art showing in it because I've been using this FineArtAmerica account for a while. In your case, when you log in you will not have any art in it yet.

The blue line beneath the word "Images" on the left indicates that you are on the "Images" page, showing your images.

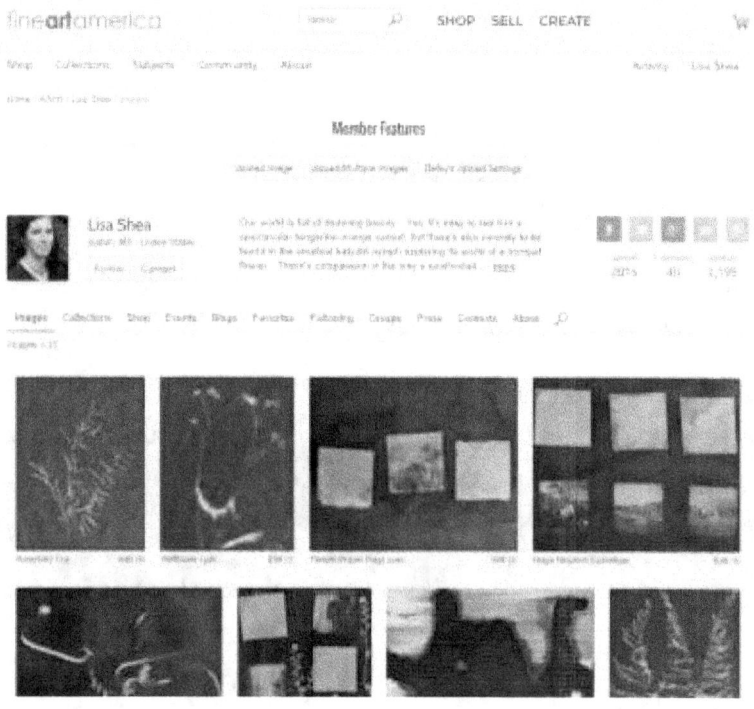

COLLECTIONS

A collection of images is simply a way of organizing them into categories. Here I have clicked on the "Collections" tab to show you how I've organized my images. You can see the word "Collections", second from the left, is now underlined in blue.

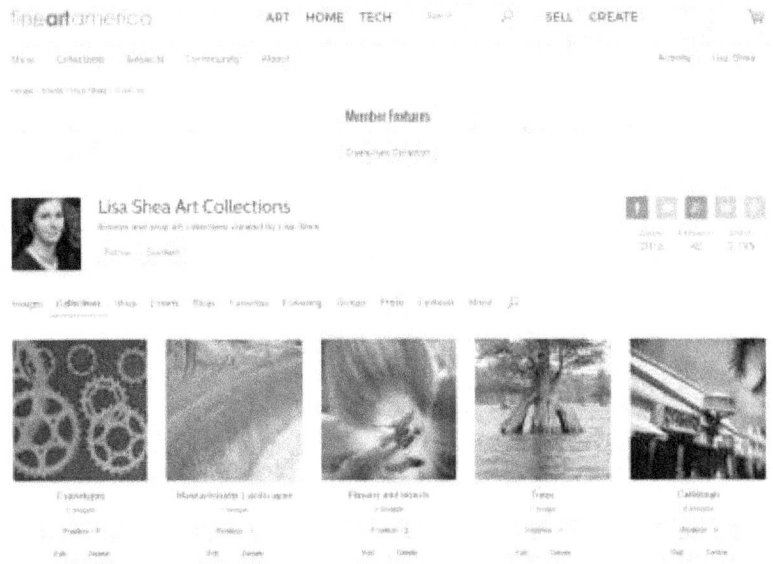

The collections I have set up are for cyanotypes, Massachusetts landscapes, flowers and insects, trees, and Caribbean. You can organize your photos any way you wish, into any sorts of collections.

If you click on one of those collections you then see all the
images within that collection. Here is what I see when I click
on the "cyanotypes" collection.

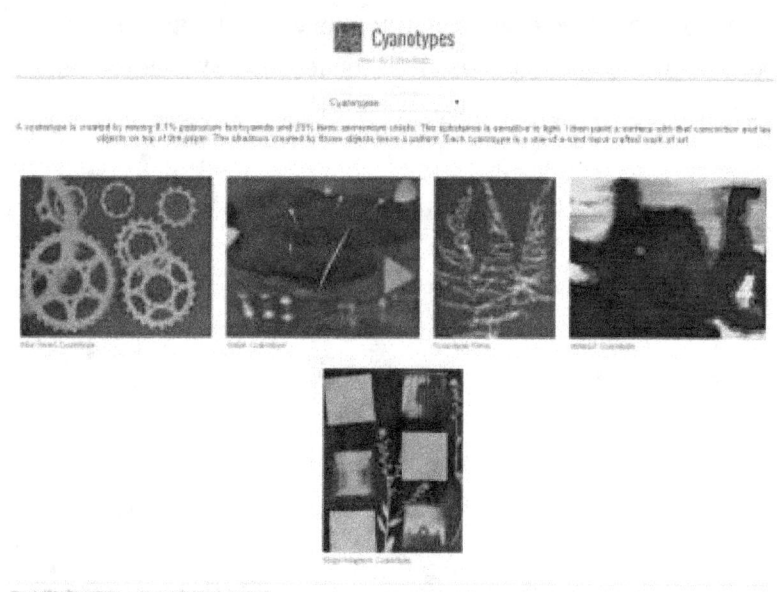

So these are my various cyanotype images. A cyanotype is a
sun print made by painting a surface (like paper) with light-
reactive chemicals. You then lay objects on top of that surface.
I use gears, ferns, and guitar items in these images. When the
sun shines on the surface it turns the chemically-painted paper
blue. Where the sun can't reach, because an object blocked the
sun, the paper remains its natural color.

In any case, each of those images is available to the visitor in a
variety of formats. They can buy framed prints, mugs with the
image, tote bags, and other items.

So next, let's see how to add an image to the fine art America website.

ADDING AN IMAGE

At the top of the profile page is a gray button for "upload image." Clicking on that brings you, naturally, to the image upload screen.

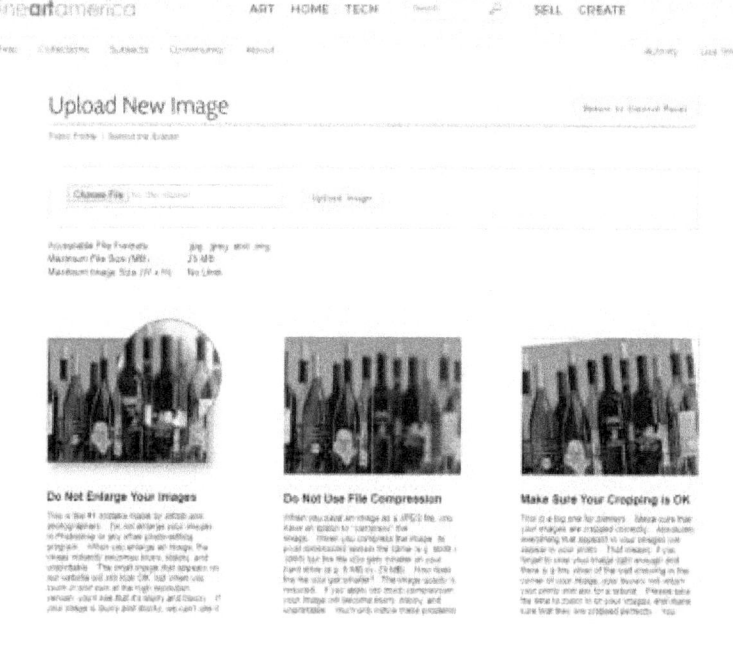

The "Choose file" button lets you browse your hard drive to find the folder which has your images. Browse until you find where you store your images, and then select the image you wish to use.

It's good to read the helpful hints below that button. They talk about how to make sure you have cropped your image properly, that you don't artificially alter your files, and so on.

Once you select your file, you're brought to a page that lets you describe this image you just uploaded. Here's the first section of that page.

The key things here are the title, keywords, and description. Make sure you use commonly searched on words in here. For example, if the image is of your mom holding a bouquet of roses in a gazebo by a meadow, don't just call the image "mom". It's unlikely most people looking for a photo with a gazebo would know to use the key word "mom". Instead, label it something like "Woman with Roses in Gazebo by Meadow."

That way when people search for Roses or Gazebo or Meadow
or so on will find it. The same is true for the keywords area.
Put in as many key words as possible that relate to your image.
The more the better. If you really want to talk about your mom
and the situation that led to the picture, use the description field
for that.

Scrolling down, you get to the next area for input.

Here you can put your work into one of those collections –
which they call here "Galleries" – that you have created to
organize your art. You can always organize your art later, so
don't worry about doing this right away if you don't have
thoughts as to your categories. You can always edit that (or
anything else here) later on.

Note the area for "Original Artwork". If this is a physical work
of art like an oil painting or a watercolor, you can offer that

original piece for sale as well. Just put in its dimensions and price.

Amazingly – and here's the link to prove it –

https://fineartamerica.com/tour/sell-originals

If you sell an original you do it COMMISSION FREE. You contact the buyer directly and arrange the rest directly with them. So that is a nice added feature.

OK, on to the things FineArtAmerica is offering for sale. There's a variety of items here that they sell for you. These include prints, greeting cards, and more. For the items that FineArtAmerica sells, they handle everything. The buyer places an order. FineArtAmerica takes the money plus shipping, makes the item, sends it to the buyer, and then deposits your share into your bank account.

You determine your share by setting the mark-up price over their base amount. You can see that here:

Print Products

Prints

Your image is 751 pixels x 906 pixels. This allows you to sell prints at the sizes below. Please specify a price for each size. We add our cost of materials (e.g. canvas, frames, mats, etc.) to your prices in order to arrive at the final prices paid by the buyers. If you do not want to offer a particular size for sale, simply leave the price blank.

Size	Your Mark-Up
6.375" x 8.000"	1.00
8.000" x 10.000"	3.00

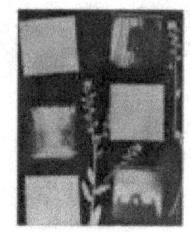

 Allow Cropping to Standard Print Sizes (Recommended)

If this option is selected, buyers will be able to crop your image to standard print sizes each as 8" x 11", 11" x 14", etc. If the buyer selects a standard print size, your image will be center cropped to fit that size. Our code will determine which of your uncropped print sizes above is closest to the standard print size that was selected by the buyer and then pay you accordingly.

Greeting Cards

In each of the boxes below, please enter your mark-up for a single card. Your prices get added to the appropriate base prices to arrive at the final sell price.

Size	Your Mark-Up Per Card	Base Price Per Card	Sell Price Per Card	Sell Price Per Pack
Single Card	2.00	3.95	5.95	5.95
Pack of 10 Cards	0.00	1.95	3.95	39.50
Pack of 25 Cards	2.00	1.50	3.50	87.50

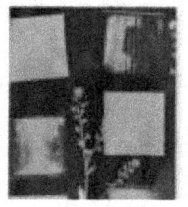

So let's take the greeting cards category. They say it costs $3.95 for them to print a single card. You can then set your mark up (i.e. your profit) on that card sale. In my example I have the mark-up set to $2. That means the visitor sees the price to buy this card at $5.95. If a visitor buys a card they pay $5.95 plus shipping to get it. FineArtAmerica prints the card and sends it to them. FineArtAmerica keeps their base $3.95 for the card, they handle the shipping, and I get my $2 profit deposited into my account.

There are many other items available like shower curtains and such – the list grows regularly. Still, compared with other companies like CafePress, the list is fairly tiny. FineArtAmerica is mostly about the nicely framed prints.

You can also sell digital copies of your work, for use in TV, magazines, and other works. You can choose to activate this option or to just leave it blank. Note that some magazines like the New Yorker do use this system in order to buy artwork so it might be something to consider.

To figure out pricing ideas, you can look at other artists' work in your topic area to see what they are charging.

Image Licensing (for sale on Licensing Pixels.com)

Royalty Free

Your image is 791 pixels x 986 pixels. That allows you to license your image for sale using our Royalty Free Licenses at the sizes below. Set retail price for each available size. This prices that you set are exactly how much you'll earn when you make a sale. Fine Art America does NOT subtract a commission. We add a 30% markup to your prices in order to arrive at the final prices paid by the buyers. If you do not want to offer a particular image size for sale, simply leave the price blank.

Size	Your Price
451 x 500	
852 x 1,888	One side of your image must be at least 1,327 pixels in length in order to offer this size for sale
1,604 x 2,000	One side of your image must be at least 2,327 pixels in length in order to offer this size for sale
3,208 x 4,000	One side of your image must be at least 4,000 pixels in length in order to offer this size for sale

Rights Managed

With a rights-managed license, you get to control how your image will be used and how you will be compensated for that use. When a buyer purchases a rights-managed license, the buyer will receive your full resolution image (791 pixels x 986 pixels). You can learn more about each type of available license by clicking on the appropriate link below. For licenses involving physical products, please enter a base price and a per unit price. For licenses involving digital products, only a base price is required. The prices that you set are exactly how much you'll earn when you make a sale. Fine Art America does NOT subtract a commission. We add a 33% markup to your prices in order to arrive at the final prices paid by the buyers. If you do not want to offer a particular license for sale, simply leave the prices blank.

Image Size	License ID	Medium	Term Length	Minimum Units	Base Price	Per Unit Price
791 x 986	Advertisement (Digital)	Online / Mobile	Two Years			
791 x 986	Advertisement (Print)	Physical	Two Years			
791 x 986	Advertisement (TV)	TV	Two Years			
791 x 986	Merchandise (Digital)	Digital	No Limit			
791 x 986	Merchandise (Large)	Physical	Two Years	\$1,000		
791 x 986	Merchandise (Medium)	Physical	Two Years	\$9,000		
791 x 986	Merchandise (Small)	Physical	Two Years	\$3,000		
791 x 986	Packaging	Physical	Two Years	\$0,000		
791 x 986	Promotions	Physical	Two Years	\$3,000		
791 x 986	Publishing (Digital)	Digital	No Limit			
791 x 986	Publishing (Print)	Physical	Two Years	\$1,000		

They do have options to auto-post on Facebook and Twitter, but I would leave all of that off. You always want to make your own posts so you can customize them properly.

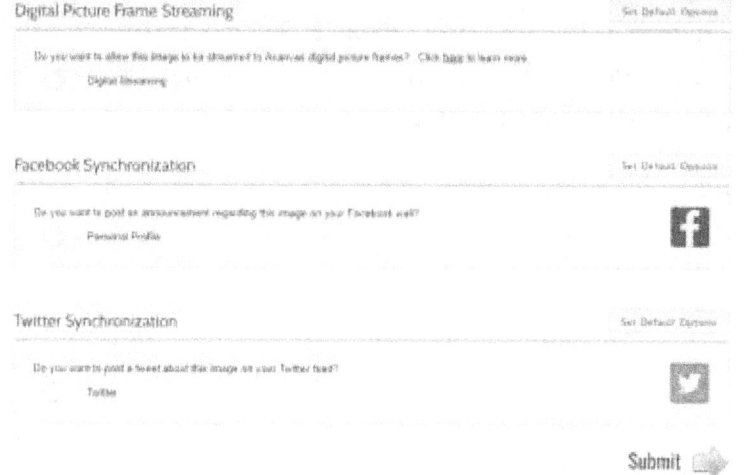

And that's it! Once you hit "submit" your work of art is live. You can always edit it whenever you wish after that.

Here is what the top of the live product listing page looks like.

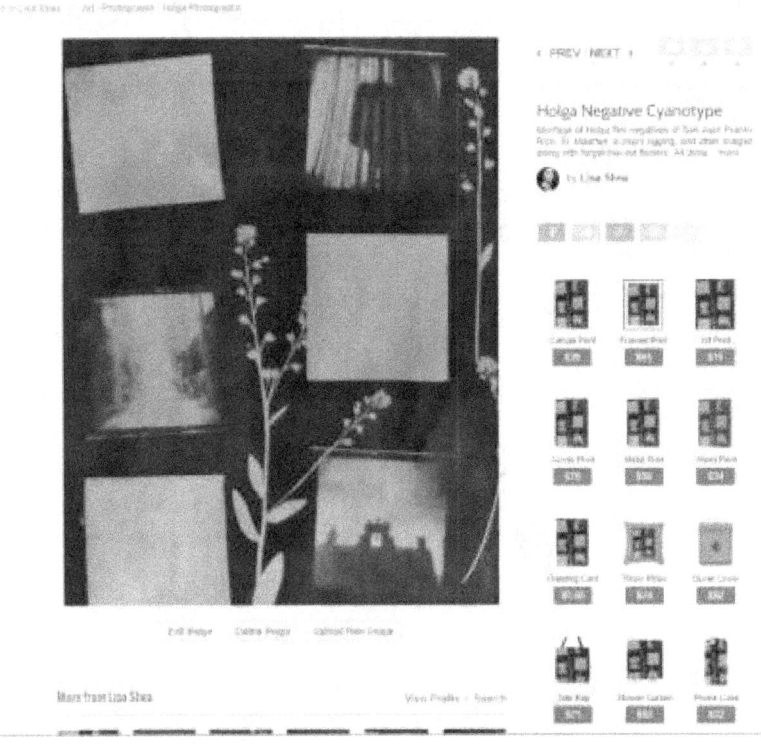

The live listing page shows a large version of the image and then on the right it shows the various options for purchase. They include canvas print, framed print, metal print, wood print, greeting cards, pillows, bags, etc.

Each price shown is the combination of the base price plus your markup.

SIZING IMAGES

FineArtAmerica is very good about helping you size your images to put them onto various objects.

Let's say the object is a square pillow. You can zoom your image in and out to get it to fit nicely on the tote bag.

So, for example, you can zoom it out so there is a colored border around the edges and you show the entire image.

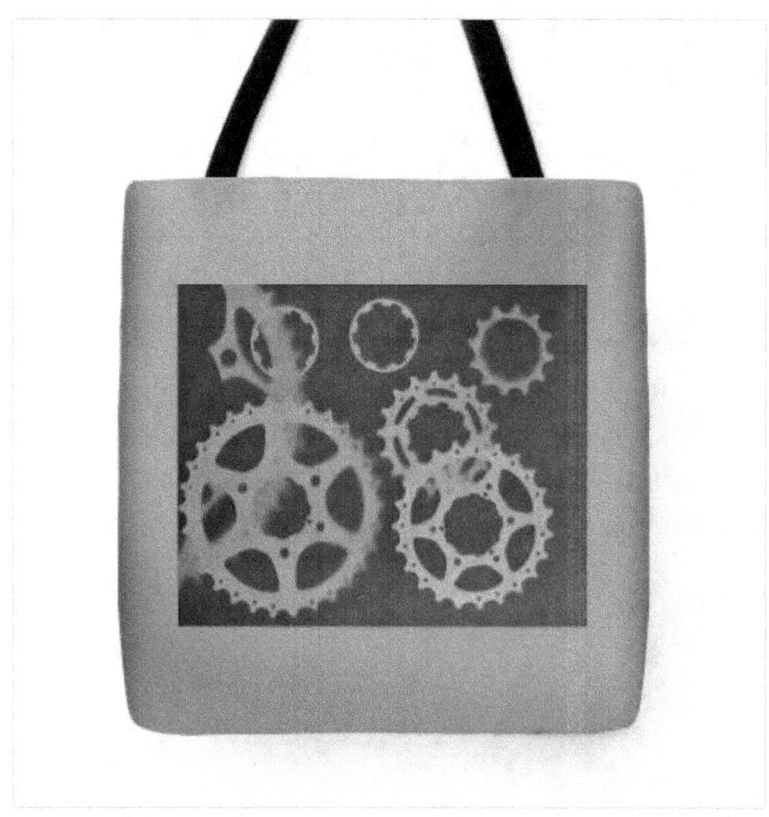

You can also choose to zoom in and chop off some edges of the image to have it fill fully.

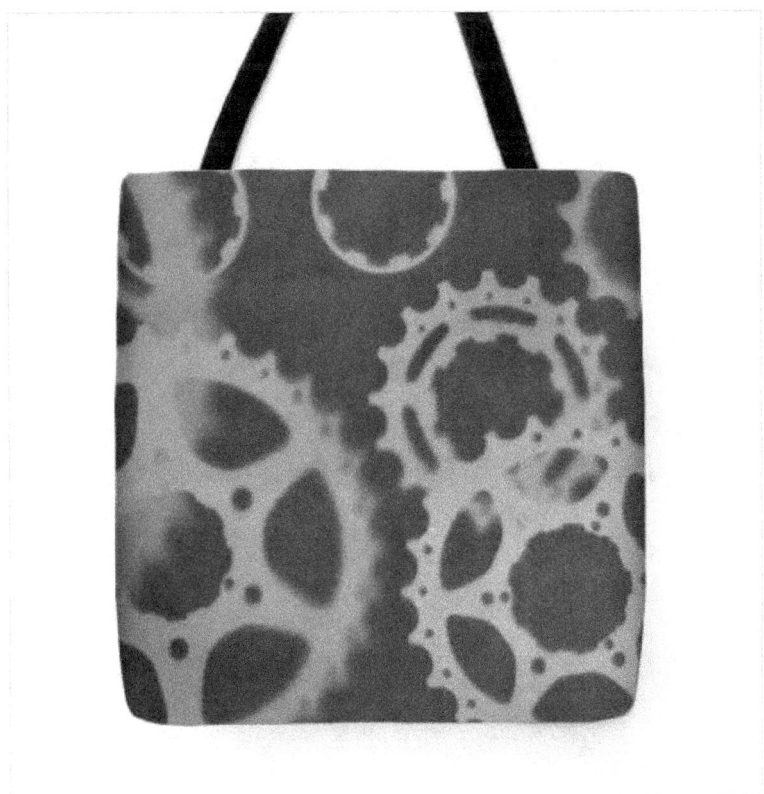

So it's completely up to you how you wish to lay out your art on the items.

SUMMARY

It's well worth putting at least your favorite 24 images for free into FineArtAmerica. It's free to do and gets you in front of a higher end audience.

CAFEPRESS.COM

CafePress is a massive repository of t-shirts, mugs, tote bags, and other inexpensive items. Thousands upon thousands of schools and clubs use this system to create club-labelled gear. As a result, lots of buyers are used to browsing CafePress to find fun gifts.

It's also a great way to create personalized items to sell, yourself, at fairs.

CafePress is wholly free to set up and use, no matter how many images you have. So you can go fairly wild in here with loading your images.

ORGANIZING YOUR IMAGES

CafePress works with the idea of having different "shops" to organize your images. In my account here you can see I have a shop for cyanotypes, one for my Sutton images, one for my medieval romance images, and so on.

It's very easy to move items around from shop to shop so don't stress too much about doing them exactly right at first. Take your best shot at defining reasonable shops, but you can always move things around later.

It's easy to make a new shop. In the top left is a green link for "Make a New Shop."

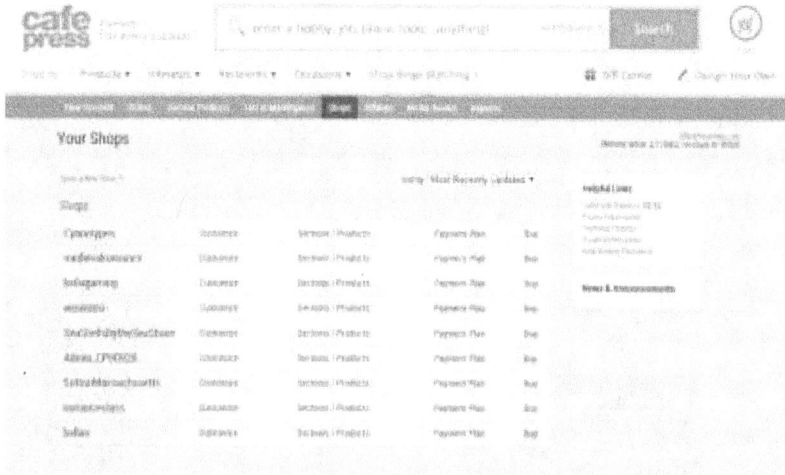

A shop would be your top level of organizing. I have a shop for my Wine items, my Sutton items, my Cyanotype items, and so on. Within each shop I have sections to organize my artwork.

As I already have a shop defined for cyanotypes. So I'm going to go in and manage that shop, to add another image to it.

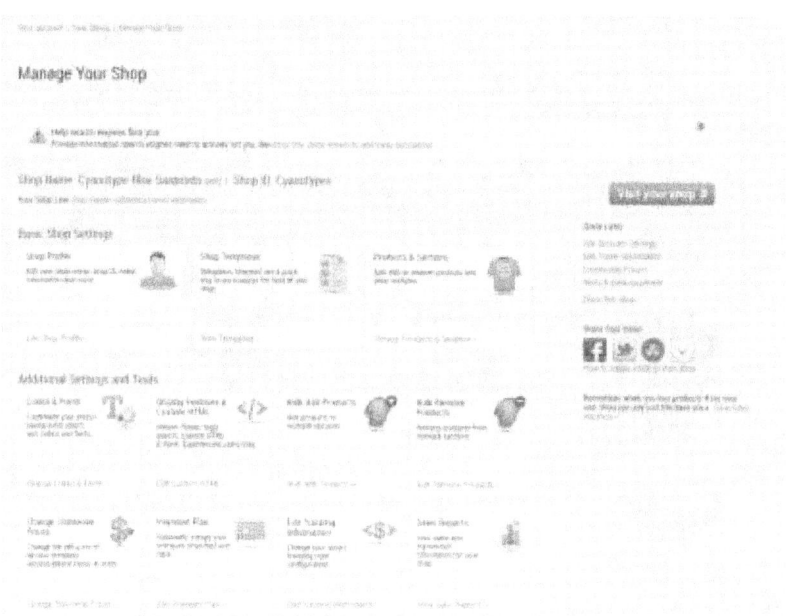

There's all sorts of options to customize the shop, but really the basic thing you will do is add new products to it. That's the link on the top right, to manage your products and sections in the shop.

Right now my cyanotype shop has four cyanotype images in it. Each image is in its own section to keep it separate from the others. Each image is available on about 300 different items from tote bags to notecards to jigsaw puzzles to pajamas and so on. Having 300 items in a section is quite enough for a visitor to deal with ☺. So it's good to have a distinct section for each new image you load in.

The sections and products page shows those four images. Each is its own section. It says, right above the images, "sections in your storefront."

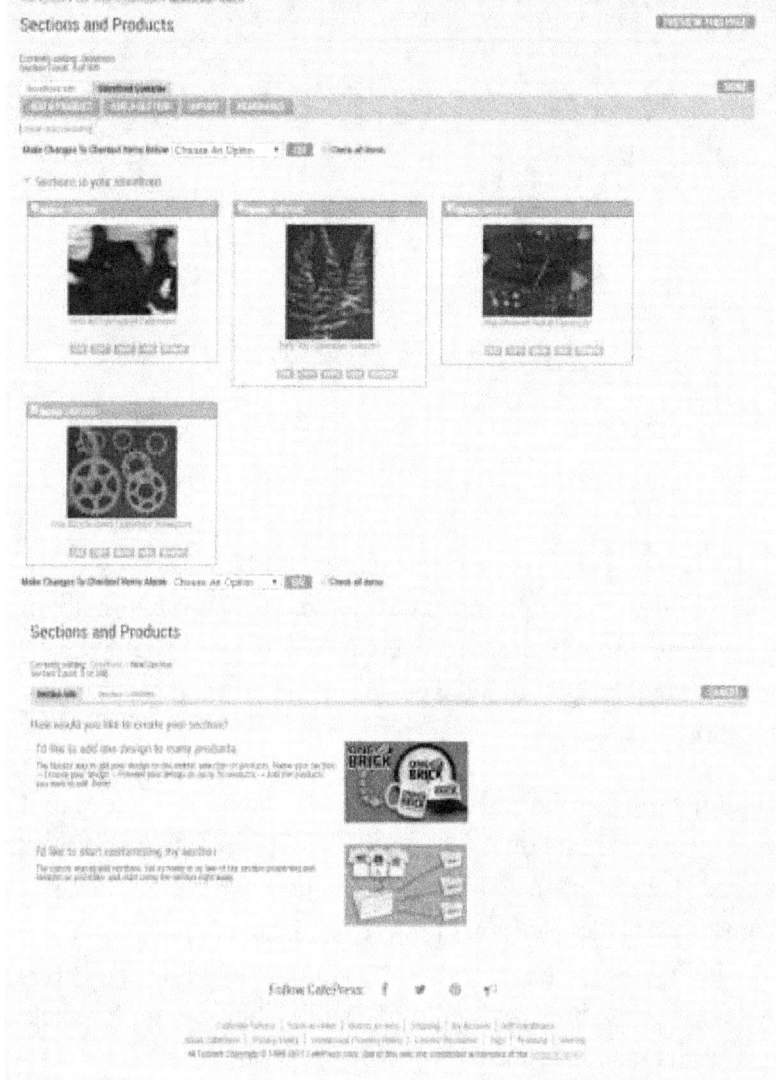

There's a gray button second from the top left to "Add a Section". This adds a new section of products, featuring an image, to your shop. So I clicked that.

ADDING A SECTION

Clicking "Add a Section" takes me to a screen for me to add in this new image and all its associated products. There's a green link in the middle to select the image in question.

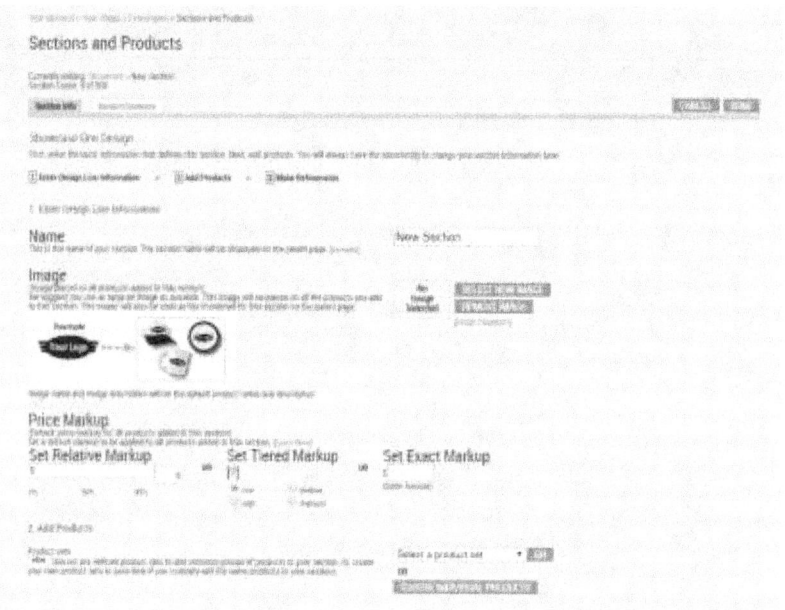

Note that you can also set the markup either in a percentage or in a set dollar amount for the entire section. That gives you a starting point for your prices. The markup is the price you charge above the base item creation cost that CafePress will get. In essence your markup is your profit.

When you click to select your image you can either select from the images you've already loaded into CafePress or you can upload a new image from your hard drive.

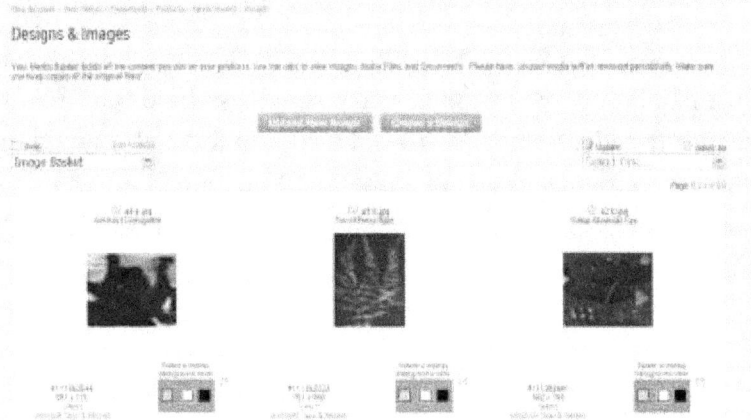

Once again, you browse your hard drive to find that image we made.

You now give this image a title, key words, and a description. Just like before, you want to make sure these fields are full of search-friendly words. You wouldn't want to label something "Mom". You would want to label it "Woman with roses in gazebo by meadow." You want to use words that people are likely to search on, that represent what is in the image.

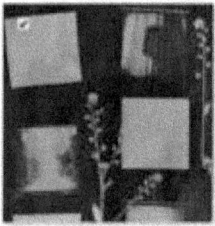

Now it's time to say which physical items you want to offer with this image. I tend to go for everything. All 300+ items from pet collars to travel mugs. I figure why not. But if you want to, you can pick and choose exactly which items you want to offer.

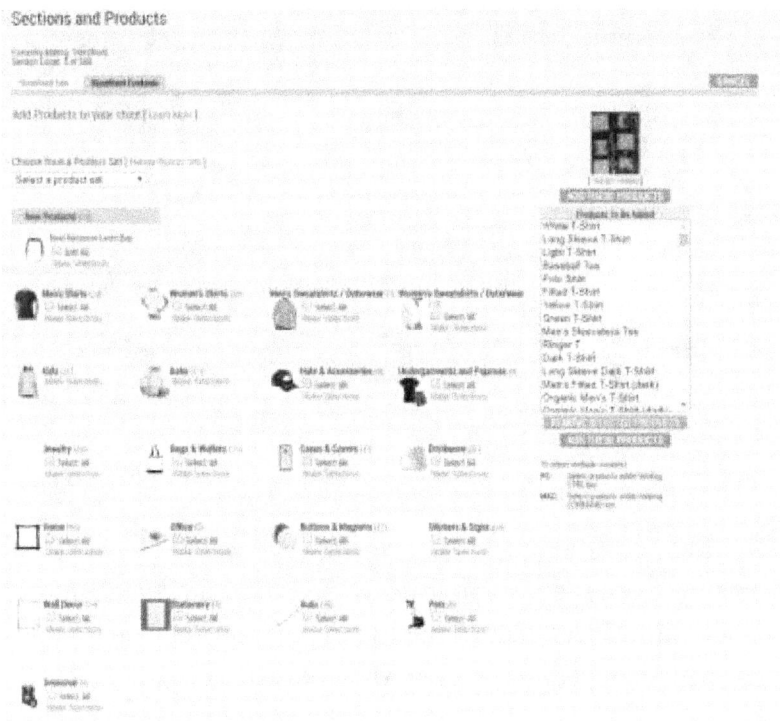

When you have chosen the products you wish to include, you click the "Add These Products" green button.

You're now shown all of those products with the image on them. Sometimes the image works out nicely, like with these t-shirts.

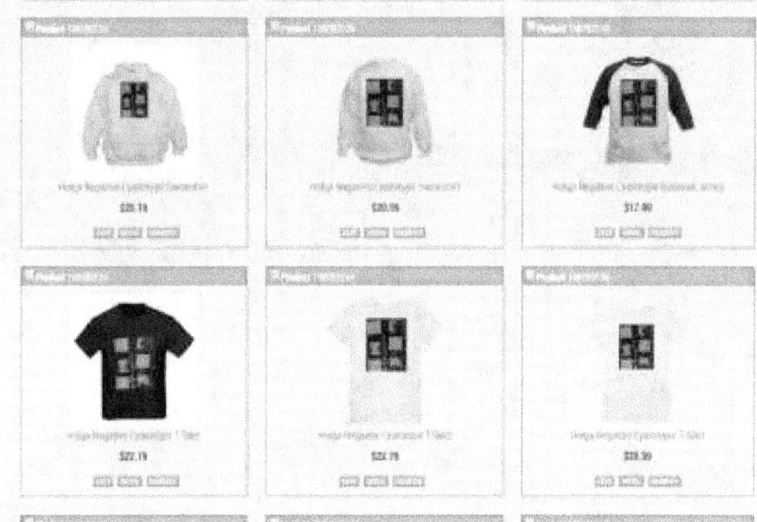

Sometimes the shape of your image doesn't quite match the shape of the object, like with these Christmas ornaments, and things get chopped off or have white borders.

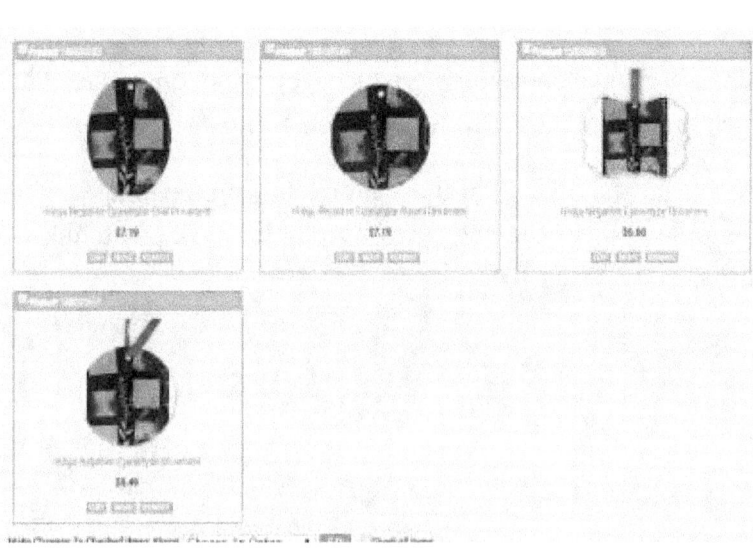

You can then edit those images to zoom in the image or to zoom it out. If you zoom in, you will lose sections of your image off the edges of the object. You can see that in the oval and round ornaments. Still, that might look pretty. For the one that looks like a bowtie ribbon, I might want to zoom it out more so there is a white border all the way around the image. Or heck I could leave it with the white edges.

If you really dislike the way your image looks on something you can remove that item from your storefront. I tend to just leave everything even if some have white borders. I figure you never know what might be interesting to a potential buyer.

You can edit every single item individually to set its markup from the CafePress base price. I tend to just set one markup for an entire section because it's easier. Usually I go with a 10% markup for the entire section. If you want to customize your markup item by item you can certainly do that.

Some items can allow more than one image. Greeting cards have an inside image you can use as a greeting. Some t-shirts have back sides you can put an image on.

The calendar lets you load in 12 images, one for each month.

So there are a few fun options in here, once you start poking around.

But for now you can just hit "Done" in the top right to save your new section. You can always edit things later if you wish.

Once your section is saved, it's live. Visitors can find it and buy from it. You can share that link with family and friends and encourage them to come and buy items. You can buy items, yourself, as the shop owner and get them at the cheapest base price.

SIZING IMAGES

Remember with Fine Art America how you could "over zoom" to get just a portion of your artwork to show on an item like a tote bag, so that you could focus on the part of the image you wanted to feature?

CafePress does NOT have that option. CafePress stops zooming in when you reach one edge of your artwork.

Let's look at an example.

With this holiday ornament, the edges are not straight. Here I've zoomed out the image so there is a white border showing on all sides.

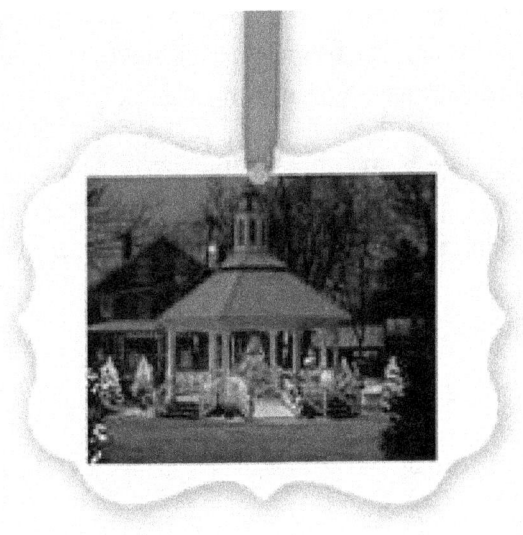

If I zoom in more, to the maximum size, this one happens to fit nicely in that space.

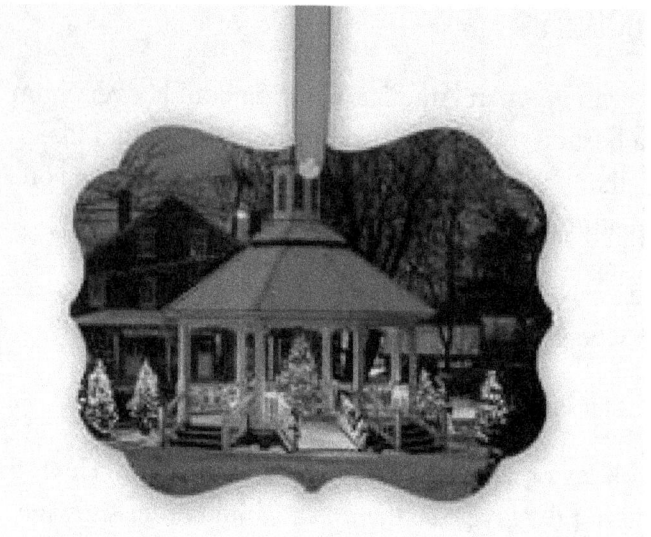

But let's say we were working with an image which did not match the general dimensions of our target object. So, in this case, something more square-proportion in shape.

This is a pillow with the same gazebo image on it. First, I chose to zoom it out, so I have the white border. Note how the white border is thicker on the top and bottom, because my image is not square?

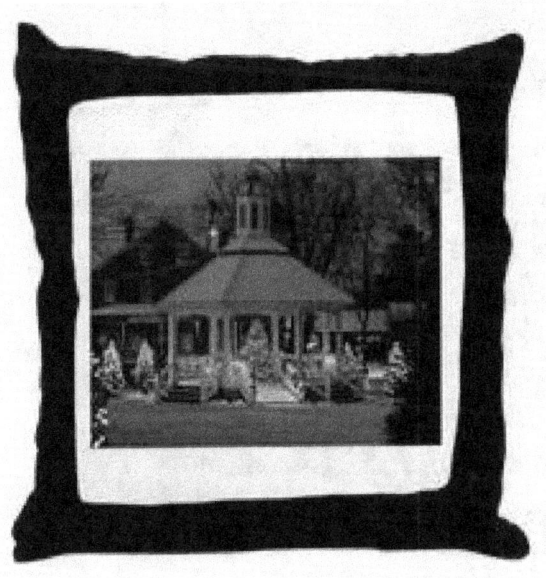

If I try to zoom in more, to get my image to fill the pillow, it stops when the left and right edges hit the sides. It won't let me "over-zoom" to feature just a portion of the image, like Fine Art America would.

Lisa Shea

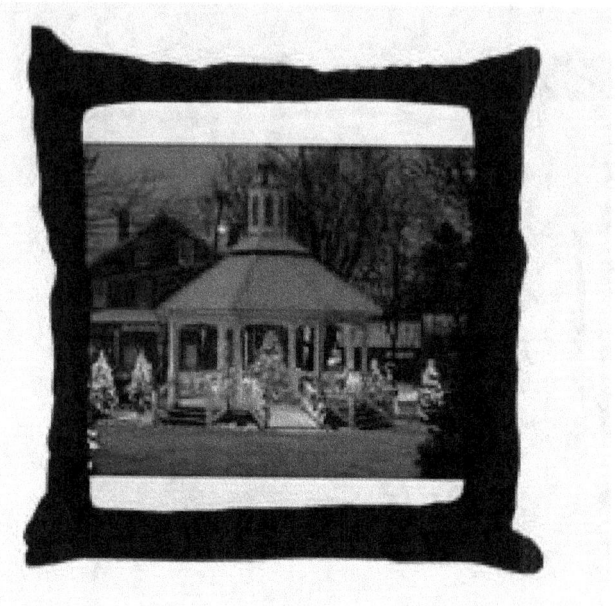

It leaves white stripes on those other two sides.

The way you have to handle this in CafePress is to do the resizing yourself. On your home computer, make a square version of your image by cropping off the edges, however you feel that crop works best.

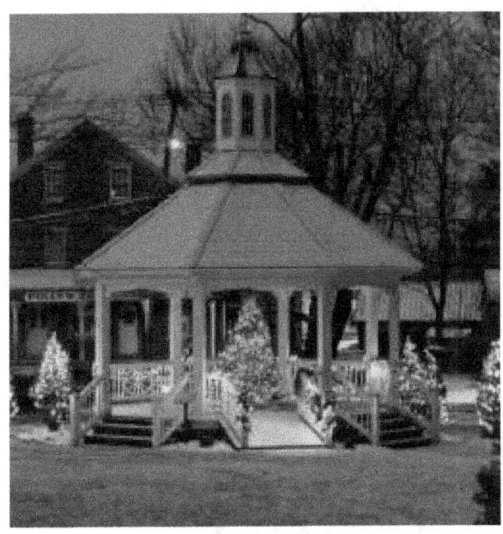

Now you can edit your section which has your gazebo photos featured. Edit the item in question which is showing up poorly. In this case, the pillow. You'll have an option there to change out the image.

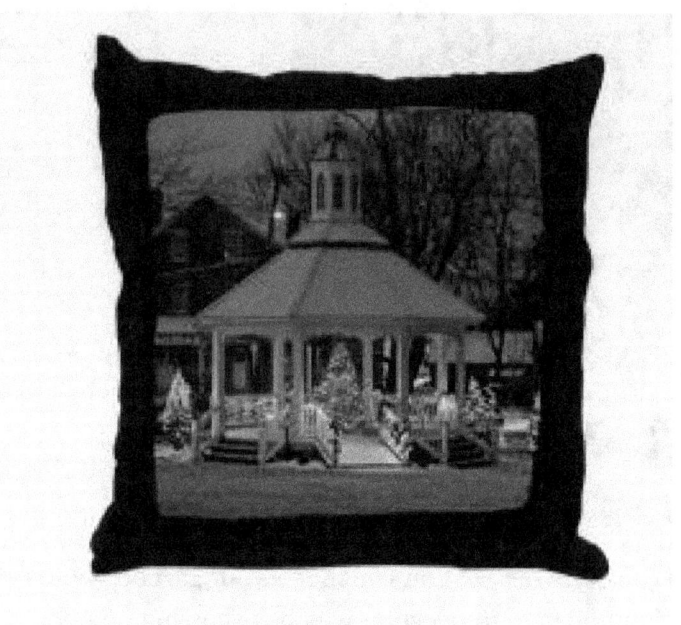

The image now looks "right".

If your image is not square by default, take a look through your store to see which items are showing white borders as a result. I would add in a square-cropped version of your image. Then edit those items and change them to using the square-cropped version. You should then be all set.

SUMMARY

Vast numbers of people shop in CafePress to buy mugs, t-shirts, tote bags, and all sorts of inexpensive things for gifts. Many artists use this system to promote their artwork and to make items to then sell at festivals and fairs.

It's completely free to use so it's worth putting your art in here – you never know who might buy it.

VISTAPRINT.COM

I primarily use VistaPrint to make business cards, and they do an awesome job with those. It's worth noting that they have some nice holiday card options.

Note that the VistaPrint interface is NOT about listing items online for sale to strangers. This would just be for you to make your own cards to then sell at festivals, art shows, or to use yourself.

https://www.vistaprint.com/holiday/christmas-cards

They have linen finish, pearl finish, glossy, matte, rounded edges, and other options. You can upload your own image to use without any modification or you can combine your image with one of their templates.

Again, it's free to design the card and then you buy however many you want. But this isn't a storefront where others could come to buy copies of your cards.

I did a test run with Bob's gazebo photo, using the least expensive option and with a half-off holiday code. I chose glossy paper. The price for 20 cards plus envelopes was $19.32 plus $4.99 shipping and $1.52 tax, so $25.83 total. That's $1.29 per card base.

I ordered them on a Sunday. They shipped on Tuesday and arrived that Thursday with basic economy shipping. So turnaround is quite fast – faster than their website ranges indicate.

The cards arrive "flat" so you have to fold them on the crease. They fold easily. They are printed edge-to-edge and the paper is reasonably thick. The inside and back is blank (although I think you have options to put text into those locations if you wish).

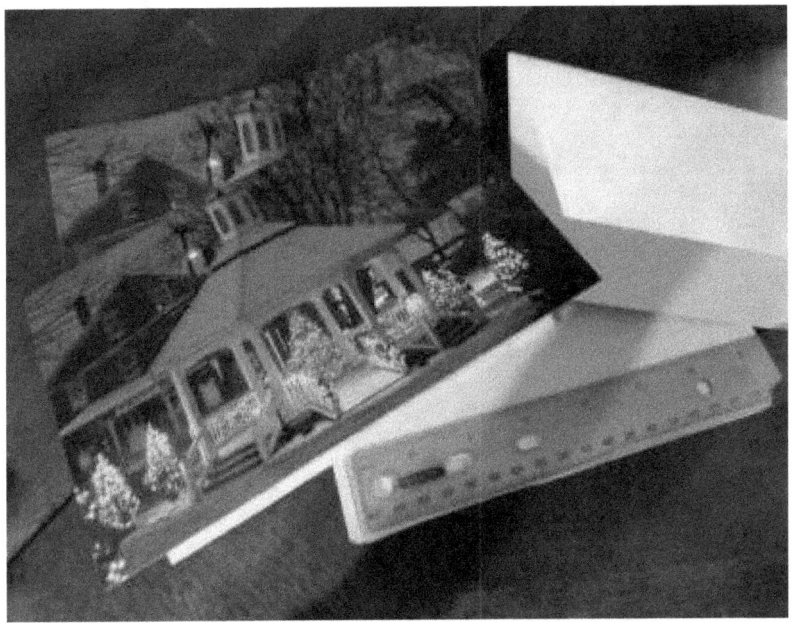

In my testing, VistaPrint is a good option and the color is crisp. Their online interface is fairly easy to use and they have some nice template options.

On the other hand, at $1.29 each base price, it might be worth looking at local options to see what their prices and quality are like.

SHUTTERFLY.COM

Shutterfly is another site for making cards, and it is also geared toward providing products directly to an end user rather than setting up a public storefront that others can use.

Still, if you want to make cool cards, Shutterfly has lots of options. They have a wealth of pretty templates. You load in your image, connect it with their existing template, and then order your batch of cards. They arrive looking professional and pretty.

https://www.shutterfly.com/cards-stationery/christmas-cards

Shutterfly isn't exactly cheap, but they have some fun options for other items, too. You can order votive candles with images printed on the outside. This is the type of place where brides go crazy ordering couple-photo-laden items for their wedding day ☺. It can be a fun resource for an artist looking for some unusual items to sell at festivals or to give as gifts.

I ordered 20 basic cards with a holiday discount code. It was $32.32 for those cards plus $5.99 shipping and $2.13 tax. That's $40.40 total, or $2.02 per card. Fairly expensive, compared with other options. That being said, everyone was impressed with the quality of the paper and printing. So depending on where you are selling your cards, people may be willing to pay the higher price for the better quality cards.

Note that I chose a feather-edge effect for this card.

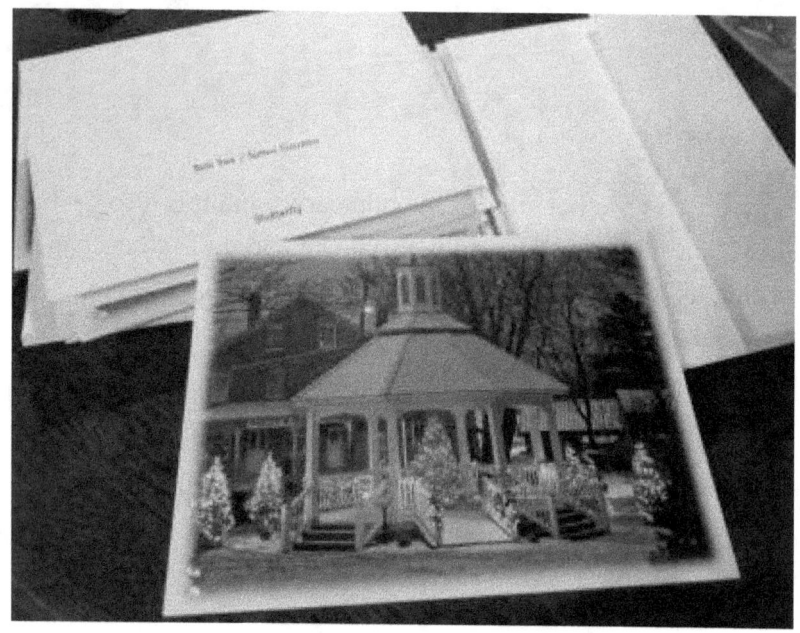

MAKING CARDS AT HOME

If you're feeling crafty, there is the option to make cards in your house which can end up being cheaper than having them custom printed as cards. Here are a few ideas.

BUYING CARDS WITH A WINDOW-HOLE

Amazon (and undoubtedly other places) sell folding note cards which have a frame-shaped opening on the front. There's a gap on the right side of the front which lets you slide a 4x6 printout into that space. So the card is really three layers. The very front, which is the outer frame. The "back of the front" which holds the 4x6 image in place. Then the back side of the card.

In this image, see how the 4x6 photo is being slid into the frame area? The "back" you see behind the photo is the back of the card's front flap. There is then still an actual back to the card as well.

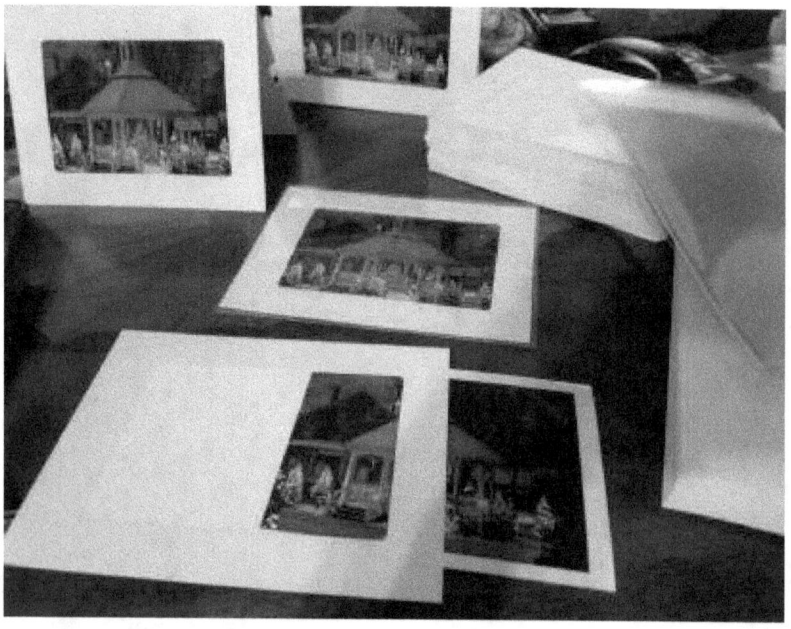

Here is the link to the framed card option.

https://www.amazon.com/gp/product/B0716S51HV/

It's $14.99 for 50 cards-plus-envelopes so that is 30 cents a set.

I then also purchased plastic bags to hold them, which you can see in the top right of that image. The finished card in the very center of the image is within a plastic bag, so it fits just right. The plastic bags are sold separately for $14.23 for 200 of them. That's 7 cents a bag.

https://www.amazon.com/gp/product/B0105Y1JFA/

You can home-print a 4x6 card for about 15 cents in ink and paper costs, or you can get those prints done from a number of local sources.

The overall base cost is about 52 cents a finished card, and the assembly is quite easy. You're just sliding photos into their slots.

GLUING PHOTOS ONTO BLANK CARDS

Another option is to buy completely blank cards plus envelopes that are larger than 4x6 in size and then to simply glue your photo to the front of it. Here you'd have to be a bit more attentive – you want to glue that photo so it's reasonably centered on the front of your card.

Here's a set I bought from Amazon. The cards are 5x7.

They're $13.99 for 200, or 7 cents each. That's fairly cheap.

https://www.amazon.com/gp/product/B071F3KCS2/

You then buy those same plastic bags to hold them at 7 cents each –

https://www.amazon.com/gp/product/B0105Y1JFA/

and if you add in about 15 cents for printing the front image on 4x6 size, that's 29 cents total for the entire construction. It does take more effort, though, since instead of just sliding a photo into a preset frame you have to carefully place it down into the center of the card and glue it there.

Still, if you're good with gluing, this is a great option!

PRINTING YOUR OWN CARDS

You also have the option of simply printing your own cards onto card stock on your home printer. They sell pre-sized, pre-creased cards that you can send through your printer. Or, heck, you can buy card stock and print on that, and then fold it by hand.

Make sure you have a good printer if you're going to embark on this process. The quality level of your printer is going to impact the quality level of your artwork.

Also, look at how much it's going to cost you in ink. Ink can be quite expensive. It could be cheaper to have someone else print them for you – they buy their ink wholesale in bulk – vs you using your commercially-bought ink to make the cards.

SUMMARY

There are a number of free options online to help you create beautiful merchandise from your artwork. Once you have that base JPG image created, the sky's the limit. You can make prints, mugs, tote bags, candles, calendars, you name it. All you pay is the production cost for the item. And if you use FineArtAmerica.com or CafePress.com, you can get other people to buy your items as well.

It's worth setting your favorite artwork items up in these stores. They then sell for you 24x7 while you work on creating more.

Enjoy!

All proceeds from sales of this book, in locations where it isn't free as intended (for example in paperback format), support childhood art programs.

Feel free to contact me with any questions or suggestions!

GLOSSARY

GIF – Graphics Interchange Format, which is either pronounced *jif* or *ghif*. The advantage of GIF is if you need the edges to be transparent. That is the main reason people would use a GIF format.

JPG – Joint Photographic Group format of file – a standard format for image files. Most cameras take photos in JPG format. Most image websites accept images in this format as well. JPG does not allow transparent regions.

Thank you for reading this *Making Merchandise from Art* book! I hope I helped you along your way to a creative new hobby!

If you enjoyed this book, please leave feedback! All proceeds benefit children's art programs.

You can also post Goodreads and any other systems you use. Together we can help make a difference!

Be sure to sign up for my free newsletter! You'll get alerts of free books, discounts, and new releases. I run my own newsletter server – nobody else will ever see your email address. I promise!

http://www.lisashea.com/lisabase/subscribe.html

DEDICATION

To the Blackstone Valley Art Association who encourages and inspires me daily.

To Cheri Roman, April Brown, Shannon Mokry, Linda Rosium, and Cecily Wolfe for their feedback and suggestions.

To my boyfriend, who encourages me in all of my dreams.

Most of all, to my loyal fans on GoodReads, Facebook, Twitter, Google+, and other systems who encourage me. Thank you so much for your enthusiasm!

ABOUT THE AUTHOR

I discovered at an early age that I loved a variety of creative arenas. I photographed everything I saw. I scribbled on notepads. I folded origami out of receipts. Rides in busses and cars would become long brainstorming sessions for epic sagas.

As I've traveled to different parts of the world, from the misty jungles of Costa Rica to the dark-soil farmlands of Ukraine, I've become even more aware of the wide range of the human condition. So many people feel trapped in tin-roof shacks or collapsing farmhouses because that is all they know. Women stay with battering husbands because life in the outside world seems beyond their ability to cope. Because of that, I donate much of my profits to charity and strive to have my art be a vehicle for change. Sometimes I take a strong political stance, seeking to showcase a situation that is in need of change. In many other cases I strive to create a sense of optimism; a sense that, with effort and perseverance, a better outcome could result.

One of my central themes is the embracing of serenity and peace. So many times precious energy is squandered on stress, guilt, or wallowing in a past which cannot be changed. The more we can find a sense of peace within us, and cultivate our energy to use in a focused manner, the more we can achieve our goals and dreams. This is valuable not only for us directly, but also for all of those around us who we wish to help and support. This theme especially shines through my soul in my many photographs of quiet, natural scenes.

Most of all, I enthusiastically strive to learn and grow every day. I am continually exploring new techniques, researching new styles, and extolling the diversity which is our world.

I actively embrace social networking and would love to talk with fellow artists and fans about the world of art. I am inspired and awed every day by what our world has to offer us.

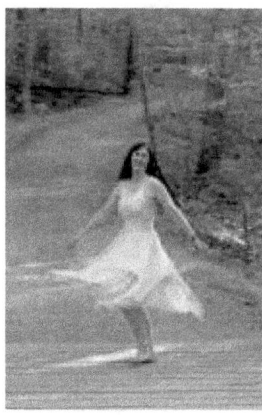

Please visit the following pages for news about free books, discounted releases, and new launches. Feel free to post questions there – I strive to answer within a day!

Facebook:
https://www.facebook.com/LisaSheaAuthor

Twitter:
https://twitter.com/LisaSheaAuthor

Google+:
https://plus.google.com/+LisaSheaAuthor/posts

GoodReads:
https://www.goodreads.com/lisashea/

Blog:
http://www.lisashea.com/lisabase/blog/

Newsletter:
http://www.lisashea.com/lisabase/subscribe.html

Share the news – we all want to enjoy interesting novels!

FREE EBOOKS

Here's my library of free books. They should be available for free on all platforms. Enjoy!

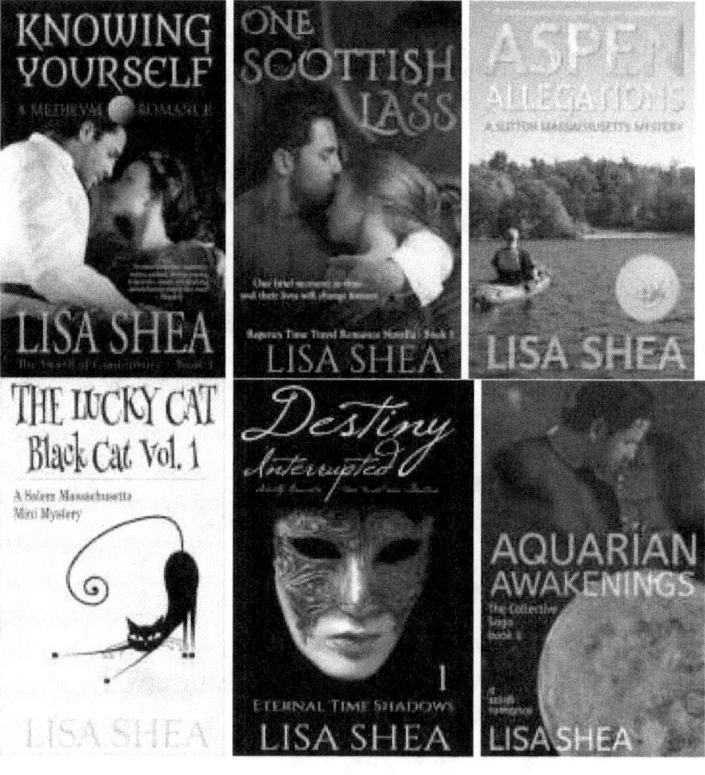

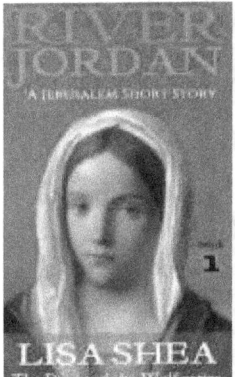
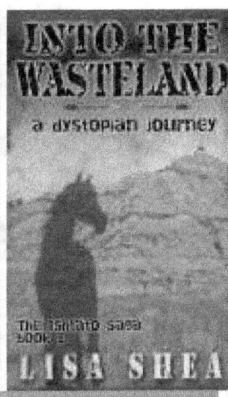
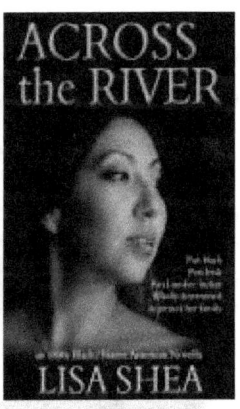

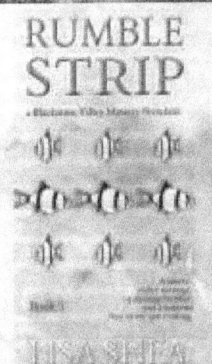
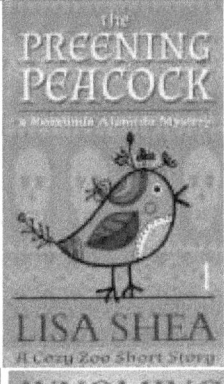
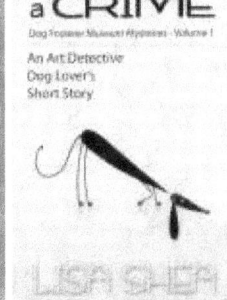

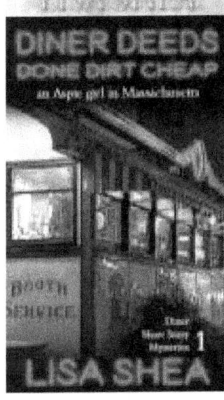
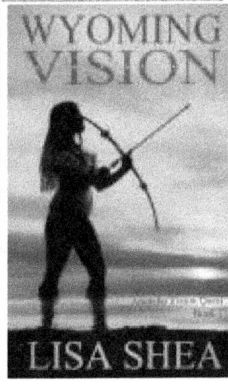
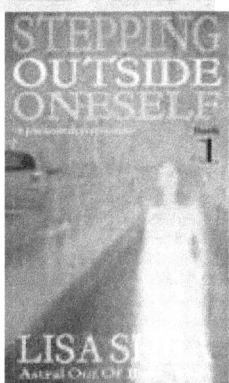

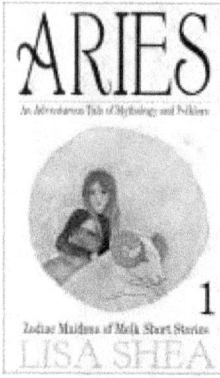

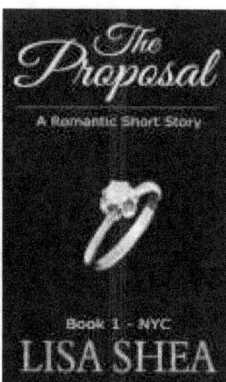
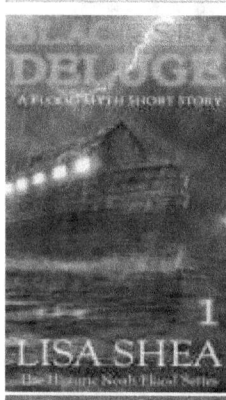
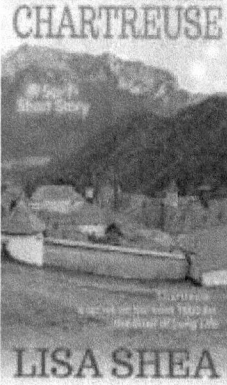
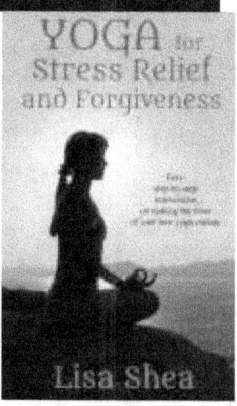
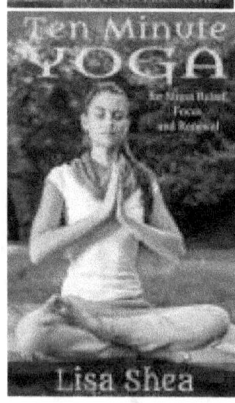
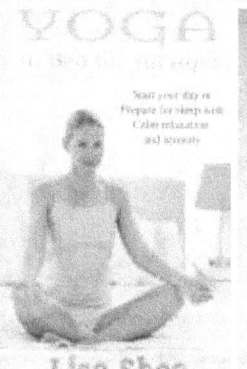
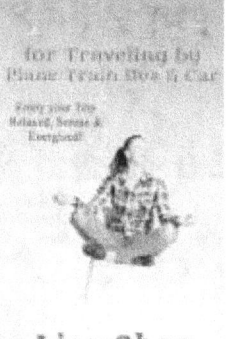

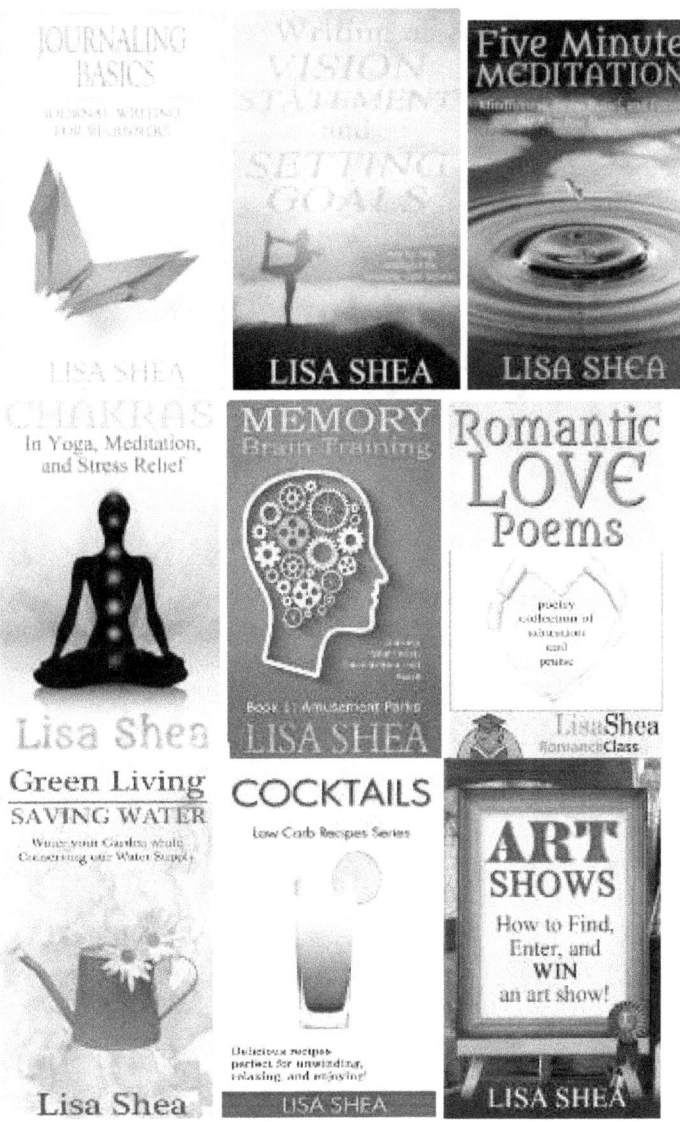

I may have added more free books since releasing this list here. For the most up to date version, be sure to visit:

http://www.lisashea.com/freebooks/

Thank you for supporting the cause!

Be the change you wish to see in the world.

www.ingramcontent.com/pod-product-compliance
Lightning Source LLC
Chambersburg PA
CBHW071216220526
45468CB00002B/623

* 9 7 8 1 9 8 2 0 0 1 8 0 3 *